P9-BXV-299

Scholastic World Cultures
THE
MIDDLE EAST

by the Editors of
Scholastic Book Services

Revised Edition

Consultant

PHILIP K. HITTI, Ph.D.

Professor Emeritus,
Department of Near Eastern Studies,
Princeton University.

Readability Consultant

LAWRENCE B. CHARRY, Ed.D.

📖 SCHOLASTIC BOOK SERVICES
New York Toronto London Sydney Auckland Tokyo

Titles in This Series

CHINA
GREAT BRITAIN
THE INDIAN SUBCONTINENT
JAPAN
LATIN AMERICA
THE MIDDLE EAST
SOUTHEAST ASIA
THE SOVIET UNION AND EASTERN EUROPE
TROPICAL AND SOUTHERN AFRICA

No part of this publication may be reproduced in whole or in part, or stored in a retrieval system, or transmitted in any form or by any means, electronic, mechanical, photocopying, recording, or otherwise, without written permission of the publisher. For information regarding permission, write to Scholastic Book Services, 730 Broadway, New York, NY 10003.

ISBN 0-590-30990-0

Copyright © 1981, 1976, 1972 by Scholastic Inc.
All rights reserved.
Published by Scholastic Book Services,
a division of Scholastic Inc.
Printed in the U.S.A.
12 11 10 9 8 7 6 5 4 3   3 4 5/8
                                                             09

General Editor for WORLD CULTURES: *Stephen M. Lewin*
Associate Editors: John Nickerson, LeRoy Hayman
Special Editor: Charles L. Wrye
Assistant Editor: Elvira Pedernales
Teaching Guide Editor: Frances Plotkin

Production Editor: Nancy J. Smith

Art Director and Designer: Irmgard Lochner
Art Assistant: Wilhelmina Reyinga
Photo Editor: Elnora Bode

COVER: A solitary Middle Easterner — overshadowed by the timeless beauty of the Dome of the Rock, a Moslem mosque built in Jerusalem 1,200 years ago.

THE
MIDDLE EAST

Table of Contents

PROLOGUE

ON MIDDLE GROUND

MUCH OF THE region known as the Middle East is dry desert. The huge Sahara Desert in north Africa touches several Middle Eastern nations. And there are other deserts scattered throughout the region. It seldom rains in desert lands. Yet when it does rain, it pours

— pelting down in torrents, turning dry gulleys into rivers of slimy mud.

Like weather conditions in the region, the sprawling lands of the Middle East can surprise you. The region occupies a lot of territory, and it takes in many peoples. There are people who speak Arabic, Turkish, Hebrew, and other languages. There are Christians, Jews, and millions and millions of Moslems. In short, there is as wide-ranging a group of peoples as you can find anywhere on the globe.

These peoples have rarely been at peace for any lengthy stretch of time. And their various struggles often make worldwide headlines. But there is more to life in the Middle East than stories which make headlines. And to understand the headlines, it is necessary to know the cultural backgrounds of the peoples.

Israel is a Jewish nation. Most of its people are Jews. In the rest of the Middle East, the majority of the people are Arabs of the Moslem faith.

Many Arabs are angry over the existence of Israel. Arabs have lived for almost 13 centuries on the land that has become the nation of Israel, and many resent the Jews as intruders. On the other hand, for the last 2,000 years, Jews have looked upon Israel as the land to which they hoped they would return one day. Some Jews, indeed, have always lived on this land.

Since 1948 this dispute has caused a handful of wars — and uncountable small, but bloody, clashes. It has further divided a region already divided in several different ways. And it has shown again and again that what happens in the troubled Middle East will affect most nations of the world.

One thing that unites the many people of the area is the name we give them — "Middle Easterners." But what's "Middle" or "Eastern" about the nations of the

Middle East? After all, those countries are either on the northern edge of Africa or the western edge of Asia.

Part of the confusion lies in the fact that the term was invented by Europeans. They used the word "East" to distinguish the region from the "West" — that is, Western Europe. The way Europeans explained it, there were two "Easts" — a "Far East" (otherwise known as East Asia) and a "Near East" (that part of the "East" which, for Europeans, was closer to home).

That all seemed very clear to Europeans.

Unfortunately, it was anything but clear to the so-called "Near Easterners" themselves. To some of them it seemed as absurd to call themselves "Near Easterners" as it would to call Greeks "Near Westerners" or English "Far Westerners." And so, to clarify the name-calling — somewhat — the term *Middle East*" was introduced.

The term has generally stuck. And actually it does make some sense. For the "Middle East" is indeed "middle" in one important way: it is a middle ground, linking the continents of Europe, Asia, and Africa and major bodies of water such as the Indian Ocean and the Mediterranean Sea.

Today the Middle East is swept up in a rolling tide of change that seems to threaten to split it apart. Some people struggle to achieve a more modern, Western way of life. Others, especially devout Moslems, seem to resent the effects of modernization. They seek to revive ancient religious and cultural traditions.

These changes make big differences in the way people think and act, the way they work and dress, even the way they look at one another. These differences, in turn, promise to create new challenges for the entire Middle East in the years ahead.

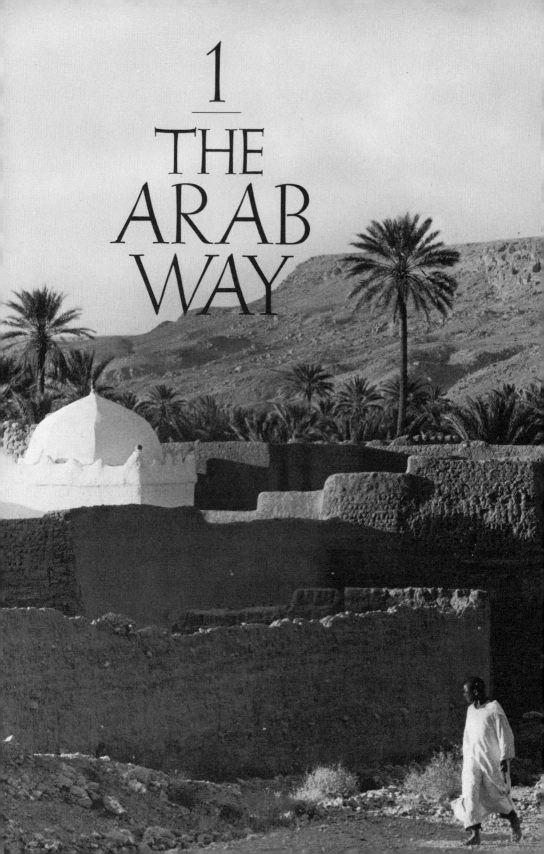

1
THE ARAB WAY

Chapter 1

The Land

IF THE WEATHER'S CLEAR, you can see the land and water from the cabin of a jet airplane 30,000 feet up.

You've left Rome or Athens headed east toward a land that has lured travelers for centuries. You skip across the island-dotted Aegean Sea, streaked with silver in the morning sun, and soon the saw-toothed coast of Turkey rises up before you. Your encounter with the Middle East has begun.

You fly east over the high, wide plateau of central Turkey with mountain ranges on your left and right. Now you're over a jumble of craggy ridges, where villages hang like eagles' nests from the mountainsides and shepherds herd their flocks in lonesome valleys. Up ahead tower the twin volcanoes of western Asia's tallest peak, Mount Ararat,* supposed port of call for Noah and his famous ark.

*See Pronunciation Guide.

Before you know it, you're over Iran. Below you lies the nation's breadbasket, a dry but fertile plateau dotted with wheat fields and fruit orchards. Your plane makes a right turn and you're in Iraq — over a V-shaped plain formed by two of the world's most historic rivers, the Tigris* and the Euphrates.* From your bird's-eye perch there seems nothing special about this plain — a fairly ordinary patchwork of farms and orchards and barren, open land. Yet it was here, more than 50 centuries ago, that restless people made the desert bloom and became the first to tell the tale in writing.

To the west yawns mile upon mile of empty desert. Political borders come up faster now — Jordan, a narrow slice of Syria, then Jordan again, and Israel. In the distance, up ahead of you, is the Mediterranean Sea, and along the coast stretches a narrow ribbon of farmland dotted every few miles with cities, towns, and villages. Below you lie the Holy Lands where two of the world's great religions — first Judaism, then Christianity — were born and a third, Islam, won many followers.

Next it's on across the Sinai* Peninsula, a triangle of desert land which links the continents of Asia and Africa. Then you come to the silent waters of the Suez Canal, a route used by some of the oil tankers as they make their way between the oil fields of the Arabian Peninsula and the shipping lanes of the Mediterranean Sea. Although you're now over Africa, the scenery remains much the same. All you can see is a blur of desert scrub and dry, rocky soil.

You'll be refueling in Cairo,* capital of the Arab Republic of Egypt, so you begin to descend. Approaching the city, your plane tilts its wings, allowing you a closer look at the world's longest river, the Nile. Here, 100 miles south of the Mediterranean, the

AVERAGE ANNUAL RAINFALL

INCHES

under 10

10 to 20

20 to 40

40 to 60

60 to 80

river is laced with bridges. Its banks are lined with boulevards. Much farther south — farther than the eye can see — lie the low, green river banks where Egyptian civilization dawned in the mists of the prehistoric past.

A dip of the wing flaps, a bump from the landing gear, and you're racing down a dusty runway at Cairo International Airport. Cairo is an ancient city, full of old stone houses and narrow, winding streets. It's also a booming metropolis — the most populous city of the Middle East and of the entire African continent.

But the last lap of your journey still beckons you, and your plane takes off again to rush you westward toward the setting sun. As you make your ascent, you approach an enormous limestone tableland called the Libyan Plateau. This tableland is one of the driest parts of the dusty Sahara — in fact, it is one of the driest parts of the earth's entire crust. In some parts it rains no more than once every 10 or 20 years.

Your jet flies on for hours across this gigantic sea of rock and sand, miles of it almost as desolate as the surface of the moon. Only now and then is the barrenness broken by splotches of green where palm trees mark the edge of an oasis.*

By now the sun is dipping low in the sky, shooting strands of light through snow-covered ridges on the far horizon. These mottled peaks are part of the Atlas Mountains, which march across North Africa from the northeastern tip of Tunisia to the southern edge of Morocco's Atlantic coast. On the far side of the Atlas is your destination: the twinkling lights of Casablanca on the Atlantic Ocean.

By now you've made a one-day sweep over most of the Middle East. You've covered nearly 6,000 miles — more than twice the air distance from New

LAND USE

Forest

Barren

Grazing

Nomadic Herding

Farming

Tropical Forest

Fishing

York to San Francisco. You've flown over three continents — Europe, Asia, and Africa. You've flown over
lands that border on three major bodies of water —
the Mediterranean Sea, the Arabian Sea, and the Atlantic Ocean. You've had a bird's eye view of a region
that is a major historical crossroads of our planet.

Most of the connecting links of this crossroads
have surprisingly similar features. Basically those
features can be placed in five main categories:

*The Northern Tier (western Turkey and northern
Iran).* The most important feature of this region is its
heavily mountainous terrain. The region's farming is
carried on within two high central plateaus wedged
into the mountains. The area's sharp-edged peaks not
only look menacing, they sometimes actually move.
In recent years, Turkey and Iran have been hit with
several major earthquakes, which have taken many
lives.

*The Fertile Crescent (parts of Iran, Iraq, Syria,
Lebanon, Jordan, and Israel).* This region gets its
name from its crescent shape on a map of the Middle
East. Its reputation as fertile farmland dates back to
Biblical times, and many scholars believe it was the
site of the Garden of Eden. Despite its reputation,
farming here is no easy job. Rains come mostly during the winter months and summers are very dry.
Year after year peasants have tilled and watered and
coaxed crops out of the land.

*The Arabian Peninsula (Saudi Arabia, Yemen and
South Yemen, Bahrain, Qatar, Oman, Kuwait, the
United Arab Emirates).* This boot-shaped peninsula
is basically a giant hunk of sand-covered rock which
peaks in the west and then tilts its way downward to
the Persian Gulf. As real estate goes, it's more valuable for the oil which lies beneath its surface than
for what little grows above ground. Though moun-

16

POPULATION DISTRIBUTION

PERSONS PER
SQUARE MILE

uninhabited

1-25

25-125

over 125

Oasis

tains exist, most of the land is parched and barren desert. Much of it is unsettled, used only by wandering tribesmen and by very few of those.

The Nile River Basin (east-central Egypt and the Sudan). The Nile is the longest river in the world. It flows out of central Africa, and tumbles around mountains and through jungles and deserts for more than 4,000 miles. As it snakes its way downstream past the southern border of Egypt, it grows more and more vital to the people who live along its banks. For centuries, the waters of the Nile have irrigated a thin sliver of land on both banks.

The Sahara (Egypt, Libya, northern Sudan, southern parts of Tunisia, Algeria, and Morocco). This tawny no-man's-land ranks as the largest desert in the world. Its 3.3 million square miles nearly equal the area of the U.S. Contrary to the impression frequently given in movies and television shows, the Sahara is not all shifting, wind-blown sand dunes. It also contains vast mountain ranges and a plateau covered with bony, bare formations of rock. Whatever it's made of, this desert is big — and growing bigger. Experts tell us it's advancing southward at an average of 150 feet each year.

☆　☆　☆　☆　☆　☆　☆　☆　☆

These, then, are the main geographical features of the Middle East — generally flat, generally hot, generally dry. If most lands of the region share any one distinctive feature, it is their lack of rainfall. Only about five per cent of the total land area of the Middle East receives enough water for cultivation. And experts believe that only another five per cent could be made farmable with increased irrigation.

Lack of rainfall makes life hard for farmers, who make up a majority of Middle Easterners. It also poses problems for most Middle Eastern nations. With so little water to irrigate the land, few of these nations manage to grow enough food to feed themselves. Most do the best they can with what little fertile land they have. But all of them must import some food from abroad.

And so the physical setting of the Middle East directly affects the way its people get their food. It also affects much more than that. It influences the way they live and work. It has helped to mold their traditions over many years. And nowadays it shapes the way Middle Easterners react to the vast changes which are sweeping across their world.

Sumerian cuneiform, etched on wet clay and baked in the sun, is believed to be the world's oldest writing system.

WHERE HISTORY BEGAN

TIME CAN PLAY peculiar tricks on people, but have you ever heard of people playing tricks on time?

What if we were to turn the clocks of time back 50 or 60 centuries — to whirl ourselves back to the dawn of history? If we happened to land in the Middle East, we might get a close-up look at the people who first wrote about their comings and goings — who, in fact, first wrote. Period.

They were a people called Sumerians.* Our knowledge of the origins of the Sumerians is skimpy, to say the least. One scholarly hunch has it that these people were originally tribesmen who roamed inland from the Persian Gulf, never knowing where their next oasis was coming from. Some time before 4000 B.C. the Sumerians reached the plain between the Tigris and Euphrates rivers and found other peoples had already settled there. After the stark emptiness of the desert, the greenery of the plain looked inviting, so the Sumerians evidently decided to stop their wandering and settle down.

Slowly the Sumerians nursed this land into a gardening spot, then made the land their home. As they did so, they laid the foundations of their civilization. They taught themselves how to tell time in 60-minute hours and 24-hour days. They applied heat to metal to turn out a wide variety of tools and implements from cooking pots to plows. They used sails to harness the wind on water, thereby getting around the need to row their boats everywhere they went.

But their most remarkable achievement was writing, and they are believed to have been the first people to do it. They developed a "writing system" of 500 wedge-shaped characters known as cuneiform.* They drew these characters on wet clay tablets, then baked the tablets until they were dry. On the tablets the Sumerians spun stories and recorded business deals. Most important, they left behind a written record of their civilization — a record which goes by the name of history.

But the Sumerians were not the only people of their time who were accomplishing great things. Eight hundred miles to the southwest, along the fertile banks of the Nile River, the ancient Egyptians were building a civilization all their own. Like the Sumerians, the Egyptians were mainly a farming people. But unlike the Sumerians, who had formed a number of independent towns, the Egyptians went beyond the local level and organized a central government.

This organization was the work of a farsighted ruler named Menes,* who united the Nile Valley nations in about 3100 B.C. Menes is now thought to have been the first Egyptian *pharaoh** (or king). He and most of the pharaohs who followed him ruled with absolute power. They were backed by a class of nobles who enforced the laws and collected the taxes. The power of the pharaohs stemmed in part from the fact that the Egyptians worshiped them as gods.

The Egyptians believed in life after death. They thought the spirit of a dead pharaoh went to paradise, but now and then returned to inhabit his body. To allow the pharaohs to keep their privileged role after death, the Egyptians preserved their bodies by embalming them as mummies. At first they placed these mummies in simple tombs, but as the centuries passed these tombs grew steadily more elaborate. Finally this custom resulted in one of the most amazing construction jobs of all time — the building of the fabled Egyptian pyramids. Several of these pyramids still stand today near the banks of the Nile.

The pyramids have long outlived the civilization which created them. In fact, both Egypt and Sumer collapsed before invading armies.

All of this happened a long, long time ago. And yet time can play its peculiar tricks. Many who have studied the matter estimate that man has existed on Planet Earth some 1,000 or more centuries. The Sumerians and the Egyptians carved out their civilizations only a little more than 50 or 60 centuries ago. So, viewed against the timetable of human life, ancient history seems — well, almost modern.

THE RED SEA REGION

CRETE (GR.)

CYPRUS

SYRIA

LEBANON

IRAQ

ISRAEL

JORDAN

IRAN

Nile Delta

Port Said

Alexandria

Cairo

Giza

SINAI PENINSULA

Neutral Zone

KUWAIT

LIBYAN PLATEAU

BAHRAIN

OMAN

QATAR

UNITED ARAB EMIRATES

Muscat

LIBYA

ARAB REPUBLIC OF EGYPT

Nile R.

Luxor

Riyadh

Medina

SAUDI ARABIA

Aswan

Lake Nasser

Nile R.

Mecca

EMPTY QUARTER

OMAN

CHAD

Khartoum

SUDAN

Blue Nile

White Nile

PEOPLES DEMOCRATIC REPUBLIC OF YEMEN

San'a

YEMEN ARAB REPUBLIC

Medina as-Shaab

Aden

ARABIAN SEA

Lake Tana

REPUBLIC OF DJIBOUTI

CENTRAL AFRICAN REPUBLIC

ETHIOPIA

N
W   E
S

ZAIRE

UGANDA

KENYA

SOMALIA

Miles
0   100   200   300   400

0   200   400
Kilometers

Double-check

Review

1. What is the Sinai Peninsula?

2. What is the longest river in the world?

3. In which countries does the Fertile Crescent lie?

4. What was the Sumerians' most remarkable achievement?

5. Who is thought to have been the first Egyptian pharaoh?

Discussion

1. This chapter points out that land and climate help "shape the lives" of people in the Middle East. Think of the ways this is true for *your* community. Then compare your community with the information about the Middle East. Would it make sense to say, "Geography is destiny"? Why, or why not?

2. The construction of the pyramids in ancient Egypt required the work of thousands of laborers, perhaps slaves or volunteers. How do you think the pharaohs got laborers to do the work? How could people in the United States today be persuaded to work on this type of project?

3. What cultural factors might make one society — such as the Sumerian or the ancient Egyptian — more inventive and creative than another? Should a culture that is highly inventive or that has highly developed technology be thought of as "superior" to others? Why, or why not? What other things might indicate the "superiority" of a culture?

Activities

1. Some students might prepare a large wall map of the Middle East for use with this and future chapters. They could use the map on page 13 as a guide. From other maps, including maps in this book, add the names of the countries and other information to this wall map.

2. Ten words in Chapter 1 are starred (*). This indicates that they are in the Pronunciation Guide at the back of the book. A committee of students could assume primary responsibility for teaching fellow students how to pronounce these words. They could do this in advance for all future chapters.

3. The photo essays near the center of this book contain several photos showing the diversity of land in the Middle East. You might look at these photos now and mark on a map the places they show.

Skills

Use the maps "Average Annual Rainfall" and "Land Use" and information in Chapter 1 to answer the following questions.

1. Barren areas are marked by what solid color?
(a) dark purple (b) gray (c) lavender

2. What do the numbers at the bottom left corner of the "Average Annual Rainfall" map indicate?
(a) average days of rainfall each year
(b) average amount in inches of heaviest rainfall each year
(c) average amount in inches of rainfall each year

3. Which of the following amounts of annual rainfall is most common in the Middle East?
(a) under 10 inches   (b) 10 to 20 inches   (c) 60 to 80 inches

4. Which of the following uses of land is least common in the Middle East?
(a) nomadic herding   (b) barren land   (c) forest

5. Judging from its name and its reputation, as described in Chapter 1, which of the following colors or designs is used to mark land use of at least part of the Fertile Crescent?
(a) gray   (b) dark purple   (c) lavender dots

Chapter 2

Tradition and Change

FOR MORE THAN a thousand years, most of the people of the Middle East have called themselves Arabs. They mean by this that they speak the Arabic language and live the Arab way of life. This way of life is much the same from Morocco, on the west coast of Africa, to Oman, almost 4,000 miles east, on the shores of the Arabian Sea. So vast is the Arab world that it's easier to list the Middle Eastern countries which it *doesn't* include than to list the countries which it does.

The Arab world doesn't include Turkey and Iran, for most people from those countries speak Turkish, Persian, or Kurdish. Nor does it include Israel, for the dominant language there is Hebrew, and the way of life of many Israelis is closer to that of Europe and the U.S. than to the Arab world. But the Arab world *does* include most countries of the Fertile Crescent,

26

the Arabian Peninsula, and North Africa. And these countries contain a majority of the people of the Middle East.

Like many other peoples around the globe, the Arabs place great emphasis on their traditions. Probably the most important influence on those traditions is religion. Though some Arabs are Christians or Jews, by far the largest number are Moslems. They govern their lives according to the laws of their religion, Islam, as do most Turks and Iranians.

This religion arises from the teachings of an Arab named Mohammed, who lived in the seventh century A.D. (see page 34). Like Abraham, Moses, and Jesus before him, Mohammed stressed belief in one Supreme Being. Moslems call their God Allah. They believe that the words of Allah, as heard by Mohammed, were written down in a holy book called the Koran.*

One passage from the Koran describes how the faithful look upon Allah. *"He is God, the One and Only; God, the Eternal, Absolute."*

Moslems believe that Allah is responsible for the differences which exist between people on earth — the differences, say, between rich and poor. Says the Koran: *"We have created you in degrees, one above the other."*

Since these differences are all of Allah's making, Moslems believe that virtuous people must accept them honorably. For the most part, Moslems are taught to accept their lot in life as fate.

According to the Koran, a man may have as many as four wives at one time. Four wives are therefore legal in most Moslem countries. The Koran also says that *"men are the managers of the affairs of women."* A number of Moslem customs are based on this rule, and in many areas they are strictly followed.

For example, in many Middle Eastern countries, the women are expected to lead secluded lives. In a traditional Moslem home, a separate area, called a *harem*,* is set aside for them. Only men who are members of the family may enter it. Outside their homes women cover their faces with veils. They avoid strangers and never go to public places such as restaurants.

Many Middle Easterners also think it is wrong for girls to attend school. Since Moslem women are supposed to spend most of their time at home, these people believe the women do not need an education.

Other Moslem traditions are also closely observed in parts of many Middle Eastern countries. Since the Koran forbids alcoholic drinks, no wine or liquor may be sold publicly in Saudi Arabia, Yemen, Kuwait, or Iran. Traditional Moslem rules forbid the showing of people or animals in paintings or sculpture. These rules aren't always observed, but Saudi Arabia and Iran prohibit movie theaters. This prohibition may have as much to do with keeping out foreign influence as with observing Moslem traditions strictly.

Not all Moslems interpret the laws of Islam strictly. Most Moslem countries allow the sale of wine and liquor, though most devout Moslems refuse it. Outside Saudi Arabia and Iran, movies are available and highly popular in the Middle East. And many Moslem artists no longer feel bound by the rule against portraying human beings in their art.

Still, the traditions of Islam continue to exercise a strong influence on Arab traditions. So, too, does the

A hint of mystery seemingly surrounds Arab women sheathed in long gowns and veils. But is this really a mystery — or is it just our ignorance of a people's way of life that makes it seem strange to us?

29

Arabic language, which serves as the "mother tongue" for more than 100 million people. For many Arabs, their language has a special significance, beyond the basic idea of conveying ideas and information.

Actually there are two Arabics. One is the written language which, as you can see below, is written in a graceful, flowing script. The other is the spoken language, which comes in several different dialects depending on the area of the Arab world. Spoken Arabic bears little resemblance to the formal, written style. Many Arabs greatly revere the spoken language, as this old Arab proverb indicates:

"Wisdom has alighted on three things: the brain of the Franks, the hands of the Chinese, and the tongue of the Arabs."

The importance placed on spoken Arabic shows up in the attention Arabs have paid to oral poetry. A century before Mohammed, Arab tribesmen listened in rapt silence while poets recited at fairs and other public gatherings. Long after Mohammed's death, poets continued to serve as speakers for their tribes, extolling virtues such as honesty and generosity and molding public opinion in many ways.

Arabic script reads "Kingdom of Saudi Arabia."

المملكة العربية السعودية

Arab poets were particularly adept at describing their desert surroundings. But their most important task was inspiring other members of their tribes to deeds of daring or good will.

Here is how one of them, a sixth-century poet named Salamah,* described tribal life in a poem entitled "Gone Is Youth":

*When wind blows chill from the North, we pitch
    our tents in the dales where drought has left ...
    stumps and brushes to burn....*
*When one comes calling to us for help, ... clear is
    our answer to him — forth start we straight in
    his cause;*
*Swiftly we saddle the camels strong and eager to
    go, and quick we set on our short-haired steeds
    the gear for the road.*

Though the great age of Arab poetry is a thing of the past, Arab reverence for the spoken language has lingered into the present. Even today, for example, Arabs attach great value to the ability to chant long sections of the Koran from memory. They enjoy listening to popular Arabic songs. In night clubs and concert halls from Cairo to Casablanca, Arab singers belt out ballads which speak directly to the soul.

Language — spoken, sung, or chanted — thus serves as a major force uniting the Arab world. Arab architecture gives this world a style all its own. In part, Arab building is an outgrowth of the Islamic faith. As builders, the Arabs have presented the world with two lasting religious features — the *mosque** and the *minaret.**

Mosques (or Moslem houses of worship) stand at the center of nearly every village, town, and city across the Arab world. Most are rectangular buildings

Arab husband leads his two wives down a city street.

✺§ "Men are the managers of the affairs of women."

with large, open courtyards in the center. At one or two outside corners of the mosque are minarets — towerlike structures. Some minarets are thin and straight, like pencils, while others curve upward in spiral shapes. In cities, towns, and villages, towers of the minarets perform a specific religious purpose. They are used five times a day by a Moslem official called a *muezzin,** when he summons the people to prayer.

In town after town in the Middle East, the elegance of the town's mosque contrasts vividly with its harsh desert backdrop. In larger Arab cities the flowing lines of these buildings contrast even more sharply with the straight, sharp shape of modern buildings perhaps right down the block. The mosques are a sign of Arab devotion to tradition. But the modern buildings are a sign that things are changing, too.

Tradition and change. These will be two of the main themes of this book. Tall buildings rise over the cities of the Arab world. New irrigation projects come to the villages. Even in the parched deserts, oil wells sprout where once only camels and goats grazed.

But even as things change, certain traditions remain strong. The people of the Arab world retain a strong love for their old values: for their families, for the active life, for the spoken word, and — most important — for the teachings of Islam.

Ancient manuscript shows Mohammed (left) and a follower resting during flight from Mecca to Medina.

PROPHET
TO
MILLIONS

*"There is no God but Allah, and
Mohammed is His Messenger."*

THESE WORDS serve as the basic creed for more than 550 million Moslems around the world today. Like Jews and Christians, Moslems believe in one Supreme Being. Moslems call this being Allah. But who was Mohammed, the prophet of so popular a faith?

His story begins in the latter half of the sixth century A.D. in the city of Mecca near the western coast of the

Arabian Peninsula. Once merely an outpost for wandering tribes, Mecca had recently blossomed into a prosperous way-station on the trading route from Syria to Yemen. Though trade made many Meccans very wealthy, it also troubled many others. By promoting trade, some believed, their city was winning wealth and power at the expense of older values such as honesty, generosity, and honor.

It was into this world of doubt that Mohammed was born about 570 A.D. He was the son of a not-very-well-to-do Meccan from the city's leading tribe. During his early manhood, Mohammed met a wealthy widow named Khadija.* He agreed to enter her employ, probably to help her manage her business affairs. At the age of about 25, he married her. Throughout the early years of the marriage, the couple is believed to have led a quiet, peaceful life.

As far as historians know, Mohammed observed at least some of the usual religious customs of his day. Those customs included belief in a number of pagan gods, a variety of superstitions, and several sorts of idols. But these beliefs disturbed Mohammed. When he was troubled, he would follow an age-old Arab practice and retreat to an isolated spot outside the city to meditate.

While he was meditating one night in 610 A.D., a strange thing happened. Mohammed heard a voice which ordered him: "Recite in the name of the Lord!" At first he was filled with terror, but in the following days and months he kept on hearing the voice. Under the steady encouragement of his wife, Khadija, he persuaded himself to begin preaching.

His sermon was simple: There was only one God, Allah, and he, Mohammed, was God's Messenger on earth. Mohammed did not claim to be superhuman or divine. At first he didn't even claim to be founding a new religion. As a prophet, he said he was acting in the tradition of Abraham, Moses, and Jesus, whom he thought to be other prophets in their own times.

He called his teachings Islam, meaning "submission to God's will." His first convert was Khadija, and other converts soon followed. Most were young people, rebels against Mecca's worship of wealth and power. By joining the Moslem movement, they hoped to return to older values such as generosity and honor.

As converts to Islam increased, so did opposition to it from the rulers of Mecca. These rulers received much of their income from pagan pilgrimages to their city. So, quite naturally, they supported the worship of the pagan gods.

Townspeople laughed at the Moslems, insulted them, scorned them. They even heaped garbage at the doors of Moslem homes. Soon, persecution was running rampant in Mecca. Then another blow hit Mohammed. Khadija fell ill and died.

Judging from the abuse he was receiving in Mecca, Mohammed decided he had won nearly all the converts he was going to win there for the time being. In 622 A.D. he and his followers packed their belongings, bade farewell to their families, and fled on a journey into unknown territory. Their destination was a northern oasis today known as Medina.*

This journey proved to be the crucial turning point in the history of Islam. Moslems now call this flight the *hegira,** or migration. They mark the year it took place — 622 — as the start of their calendar, just as Christians mark the birth date of Jesus as the start of theirs.

Unlike Mecca, Medina proved to be fertile soil for the growing faith. Islam quickly attracted a wide following, and Mohammed almost immediately became the leader of the entire community.

During the next few years Mohammed steadily gained the confidence of his new community. As he did so, he followed the usual Arab custom of taking several wives at once.

Mohammed proved himself an astute lawmaker, setting rules on matters ranging from inheritance to diet. He also proved himself expert at military affairs. Under his direction, the Moslem community staged a number of successful raids on passing caravans. One success led to another until the Moslems were ready to retake Mecca, which they still regarded as their spiritual home.

In 630 Moslem armies laid siege to the city. The Meccans were in no mood for fighting, and the city fell with little bloodshed.

Within the next two years, most of the Arabian Peninsula fell to Islam. Mohammed reigned as the undisputed religious leader of this desert world.

In 632 he fell ill and died. According to tradition, the news of his passing was made public by his closest friend. "If you are worshipers of Mohammed, know that he is dead," the friend is believed to have said. He added: "If you are worshipers of God, know that God is living and does not die."

It was a fitting farewell. For Mohammed had repeatedly stressed that he was God's *Messenger* and nothing more. Today Moslems sometimes wince when outsiders refer to their religion as "Mohammedanism," thereby seeming to place Mohammed in a divine role. To Moslems their prophet was simply a man who heard God's calling and spread it far and wide.

Double-check

Review

1. What areas does the Arab world include?

2. Why may alcoholic drinks not be sold publicly in Saudi Arabia?

3. When and why are minarets used?

4. What "sermon" did Mohammed preach?

5. What does *Islam* mean in English?

Discussion

1. The Arab world observes many traditions. To what extent are these traditions from before the time of Mohammed? To what extent are the traditions a result of the influence of Islam? Why do you suppose that Moslem traditions are observed more strictly in some parts of the Arab world than in other parts?

2. In Saudi Arabia, boys and girls attend separate schools. Male teachers cannot teach female students, except by closed-circuit television. Why do you suppose this is so? What are the advantages and disadvantages of such a system? Why do you think public schools in the United States are co-ed? What, if anything, does this difference suggest about different attitudes toward education in the two countries?

3. Do you agree with the Moslem belief that people should passively accept their lot in life? What people you know accept this idea? What people you know do *not* accept this idea? How might the second group of people be different if they did accept this idea?

Activities

1. Someone of the Moslem faith might be invited to speak to the class. Students could prepare questions to ask the speaker about the religious beliefs and practices of Islam on such subjects as prayer, gender roles, diet, and education.

2. Some students may wish to make drawings or models of a mosque, using examples found in an encyclopedia or a picture book. When finished, students could display the art projects in the classroom.

3. Several students might pretend to be early followers of Mohammed and write letters to their families in 622 A.D., telling them why they are fleeing Mecca and urging them, for reasons the students state in their letters, to convert to Islam.

Skills

March 1976–February 1977

Page 964   **SAUDI ARABIA** — *Continued*

Industries

Aladdin's troubled dream. J. Flanigan. il Forbes 117:28-32+
F 15 '76

Saudi slowdown hits U.S. builders. Bus W p35-6 S 20 '76
See also
Petroleum industry — Saudi Arabia

SAUDI ARABIAN pottery. See Pottery, Saudi Arabian

SAUDIA (airline) See Airlines — Saudi Arabia

SAUGUS, Mass.
Don't bury garbage, generate tax revenues, B. Forestell. il Am
City & County 91:51-4 My '76

SAUNA
Some like it hot: steam bath vs sauna. C. Duhé. Am Home
79:10+ N '76

Abbreviations   il — illustrated

F — February   + — continued on later pages

My — May   Bus W — *Business Week*

N — November   Am Home — *American Home*

S — September   Am City & County — *American City & Country*

Use the above material from Readers' Guide to Periodical Literature
and information in Chapter 2 to answer the following questions.

1. In which of the following publications will you find the articles listed
in *Readers' Guide?*

    (a) newspapers   (b) magazines   (c) books

2. How many articles are listed above?

    (a) four   (b) five   (c) seven

3. How long a period of time is covered by this edition of *Readers' Guide?*

    (a) one year   (b) two months   (c) two years

4. Under which letter of the alphabet would you look in *Readers' Guide*
for listings of articles about Saudi Arabian pottery?

    (a) A   (b) C   (c) P

5. In which magazines are articles which might relate to information in
Chapter 2?

Chapter 3

Desert Dwellers

HASSAN* IS 16 years old. In those 16 years, he has slept under a solid roof only once or twice. His home has been a "house of hair" — a tent made of cloth woven from black goat's hair. He has never been to school, and he cannot read or write. But he can hunt, and he can ride a camel or a horse. He can find his way where there are no roads, trees, mountains, lakes, or rivers — in fact, where there are no landmarks of any kind. Alone in the wilderness except for his camel, he knows how to survive.

Hassan is a Bedouin* who lives by wandering from place to place. His home is a part of Saudi Arabia called the Empty Quarter. Mostly barren and forbidding, it is one of the largest deserts in the world.

Like all Bedouins, Hassan belongs to a tribe. He is a member of the Murrah* tribe, which probably

dates back before the time of Mohammed. Murrah tribesmen are camel-raisers who wander in the desert with their herds, never staying very long in one place. When they need a fresh supply of water or their camels need a greener pasture, they pack their belongings and change camp.

The Murrah is a large tribe of about 6,000 people. It is divided into many small groups of families who travel about with their herds. Each group of families is a *clan*. In Hassan's clan there are 25 families, all related to one another. All these families live in tents similar to Hassan's.

Hassan's mother, Amina,* wove the cloth for her family's house of hair. She also made the long curtain which divides the inside of the tent into two sections. One side is for the men; the other, for the women. On the men's side, Hassan's father, Abdullah,* entertains male guests who come to the tent. On the other side of the curtain is the harem, where Hassan's mother and his two sisters live.

In the evening — unless there are male guests — the family has its main meal together in the harem. Only men who are members of the family are permitted in the harem. If Abdullah has male guests, the men dine in their own part of the tent. The women never leave the harem if there are strangers in the men's part of the tent.

Summer months are dry in the desert, and tribesmen must stay close to the villages and the wells. In late October, the rains begin again, and the clan begins its travels. After the ground has been moistened by showers, patches of green sprout in the sand. All winter long the Bedouins and their herds follow these showers.

In winter the clan changes its camp about every 10 days. By that time the camels have usually eaten all the grass around the campsite, and the sheik,* the chief of the clan, guides his people to another site. He tries to find an area where rain has recently fallen and grass has just sprouted. As long as the camels have fresh grass to eat, they can go without water for several days — much longer than can human beings or other animals. However, about every fifth day or so, the camels will also need water to drink. Then the clan must be sure that they can get to a well or a stream.

The sheik often holds a meeting in his tent with the other older men of the clan to talk over the problem of finding water and grass. Any elder may offer advice or give his opinion, and the sheik will listen with attention. Arabs have great respect for older men and believe that age and experience bring wisdom and skill.

Hassan helps in many ways with the work of the clan, mostly by caring for the camels. Selling and trading camels is the clan's way of making a living. The camels also supply much of what the Bedouins need for their daily lives: milk to drink; hair to make the cloth for tents and clothing; and hides to make sandals, waterbags, and many other useful items. Sometimes camels also provide meat, although the Bedouins seldom kill such extremely valuable animals for food.

So far this year the rains have not been plentiful, and grass and water have been hard to find. There is talk in the clan that they may face a drought — a period of no rain at all — in the next few months. The sheik heard warnings of a drought on his transistor radio, the only one in camp. Until the sheik bought his radio, the Bedouins heard news of events outside the clan only when they visited the villages or met other tribesmen at the wells.

☙ If Abdullah has male guests, the men dine in their own part of the tent, while the women remain in the harem.

Often in the evening Abdullah visits the sheik's tent with the other clansmen. There they gather to relax and talk, and enjoy their favorite drink, coffee.

On this night, the sheik reports that a new grazing place has been found which should last the camels about two weeks. But the water nearby is brackish — fit for the animals, but too salty for human beings. This means that the clan will have only camel's and goat's milk to drink. No one is too bothered, for they have often gone without water before. The men linger over the coffee, drinking three cups each, and talking long into the night.

☆ ☆ ☆ ☆ ☆ ☆ ☆ ☆ ☆

During the rainless summer, Bedouin tribes live near the settlements. Members of different tribes meet, and the Bedouins visit their friends among the town-dwellers. Also during the summer months the Bedouins do most of their trading.

Early in the morning on market days Bedouins throng the roads leading to town. For trading they bring camels, sheep, goats, hides, wool, and the rugs and cloth made by the women.

In the village square where the market is held, the merchants arrange their wares on the ground and squat beside them. Tools, water jars, cooking utensils, daggers, medicines, candy, clothing, and many other items are on display.

Bedouin men (top right) relax over coffee. Bedouin women (bottom right) tend to children in their harem.

✑ Faster and faster, Hassan's world is disappearing.

When a customer approaches, the seller does not name a price. Instead, the buyer makes an offer. The merchant, praising his wares highly, states a higher amount. This bargaining goes on and on until a price is finally agreed on and the trade is made. Arabs love to bargain and to be able to boast of how cheaply they bought a valuable item.

The most important event before the coming of the winter rains will be Hassan's wedding to Fatimah,* one of his many cousins. By the time the wedding takes place she will be 15. Bedouin girls usually do not marry much later than that.

Abdullah and Fatimah's father have already met to decide on what the marriage contract terms will be. One of these is the amount of the *mahr,* the gift which must be given by the groom to his bride. Hassan will pay his mahr in the form of animals — camels, sheep, and goats — which his father will give him.

The parents of Hassan and Fatimah were the ones who decided that the two young people should be married. Some brides never even see their future husbands until the day of the wedding. Many Arabs, especially Bedouins, still follow this custom. But many others, especially in the cities, have greater freedom to choose their own mates by themselves.

After the mahr has been paid, the wedding festivities will begin. There will be four separate celebrations. Not only will the families of the bride and groom celebrate separately, but the men and women of each family will have their own separate feasts.

When the male guests have assembled, the ser-

Workers at Arabian oil refinery head home at end of day.

vants will bring in trays of lamb stuffed with rice. Everyone will help himself from these dishes, dipping in with the fingers of his right hand (the left hand is considered unclean). Then the men will celebrate long into the night.

On the other side of the tent curtain, in the harem, Amina and all the women guests will also be feasting and celebrating. They will not join the men. According to Moslem custom, men and women do not mingle at such large gatherings.

The wedding celebrations in the tents of the two families may last as long as three days. Finally Hassan will take his bride home to his family's tent, and the wedding will be over. After his wedding, Hassan will have several camels and many sheep and goats of his own, presents from his family and Fatimah's. When the sheik calls a meeting of the men of the clan, Hassan will sit with them. As a married man, he will join the other men of his clan as an equal.

☆　☆　☆　☆　☆　☆　☆　☆　☆

Faster and faster, Hassan's world is disappearing. All over the Middle East, the number of wandering herdsmen grows smaller each year. New discoveries and developments, such as new sources of water and modern means of transportation, are changing the face of the desert itself.

Once camels were the only means of crossing the vast deserts of the Middle East. Now airplanes, helicopters, jeeps, and trucks are replacing the old camel caravans. Camels, no longer so vital to trade, no longer bring a high price in the markets. Except for the Bedouins, few people need them nowadays. Today sheep, which provide most of the meat eaten in Saudi Arabia, are more important in the marketplaces than camels. The day may soon come when a person cannot earn a living by raising and selling camels. Already many Bedouins are being forced to leave the desert and take up some other work.

In Saudi Arabia, one of the main reasons why the life of the Bedouins and all the other people is changing is oil. Although it was discovered in the Arabian Peninsula as recently as the 1930's, Saudi Arabia has since become one of the great oil-producing countries of the world. With a population of more than nine million, Saudi Arabia each year earns as much as 50 billion dollars from its oil (see Chapter 12).

Hassan may some day decide to give up the desert and work at one of the many new jobs in the oil industry. The area through which his tribe travels is close to the oil center of the country.

Some Bedouins have not been willing to give up their old life completely. But many have compromised. During the winter they pasture their animals on the desert. When the summer comes they move to the cities. Some members of the family may live near the city all year round.

Many Arabs whose families have lived for centuries in cities are proud to claim Bedouins as ancestors. The Bedouins' nomadic way of life seems destined to disappear, but it will certainly not be forgotten.

Double-check

Review

1. What is Hassan's tent made of?

2. Which is the driest season in the desert?

3. With what useful things do camels provide Bedouins?

4. What is a *mahr?*

5. What forms of transportation are replacing the old camel caravans in the desert?

Discussion

1. What would you miss most about your present life-style if you became a nomad? What would you enjoy most about being a nomad? In what ways, if you became a nomad, would your attitudes be changed toward the importance of family, education, land ownership, and government?

2. Hassan and Fatimah's marriage was arranged by their parents. What might be the advantages and drawbacks of this type of marriage? How successful do you think these arranged marriages are? Would you want your parents to pick a marriage partner for you? Explain your answers.

3. Middle Eastern countries such as Saudi Arabia are becoming modernized. More industries are being developed, and cities are growing larger. How might these developments affect the Bedouins' nomadic way of life? Their clan organizations? Their arranged marriages and other customs? Would the changes be for the better, or for the worse? Why?

Activities

1. Some students might look in magazines, newspapers, and other sources for pictures of Bedouins and the nomadic way of life on the desert. They could arrange a bulletin board display on the subject.

2. Some students might want to research one of the following aspects of the natural history of the desert: animals, birds, insects, plants, rainfall patterns, or soils. Students could give oral reports on their subjects to the rest of the class.

3. Several pairs of students could role-play a merchant and a customer in an Arab market. Use items in the classroom as the "merchandise" and spread them on the floor or on a desk. Then the "customer" and the "merchant" bargain until they agree on a price. Have the class vote on which student got the best deal.

Skills

THE WORLD'S LARGEST DESERTS

Name	Area (in thousands of square miles)	Location
Sahara	3,320	Northern Africa
Gobi	500	Mongolia and China
Rub al-Khali (Empty Quarter)	250	Arabia
Gibson	250	Western Australia
Great Victoria	250	Western and Southern Australia
Kalahari	225	Southern Africa

Source: The World Almanac

Use the table above and information in Chapter 3 to answer the following questions.

1. What does this table give information about?

2. Where did the information in this table come from?

3. How large is the Gobi Desert in area?

4. Which two deserts are located in Australia?

5. What is the Arabic name of the desert in which the Murrah tribe lives?

Chapter 4

Farmers of the Nile

IT IS A BRIGHT MORNING in a land where the sun shines steadily and summer seems to last all year. Along a road lined with palm trees, farmers walk to the fields. Because of the heat, the farmers are bare-chested and barefoot and wear only skirt-like garments which reach to their knees. On their shoulders they carry long-handled hoes made entirely of wood, even to the pointed tips.

Close to the road flows the longest river in the world, the Nile. All the water the people have comes from this river, for it rains here only two or three days a year. Without the Nile, there would be no water to drink, no water for the crops. Without the river, there would be little life.

This is Egypt, and the people are Egyptian farmers of the Nile valley.

Just beyond the village lie fields of wheat, melons, and vegetables. Beyond the fields lies the desert, the home of the Egyptian Bedouins. In the past, the Bedouins and the villagers were on less than friendly

*Mud-walled houses and shops cluster
together tightly along the narrow, twisting
streets of a village in the Nile River valley.*

terms, for the Bedouins used to make it a practice of raiding the village for food. So, for protection, village leaders long ago built a high wall around their settlement. The wall still stands, and inside it houses and shops are clustered together along narrow, winding streets.

In this village lives a 14-year-old girl named Fawzia.* Her father, Ahmed,* farms a plot of ground a little more than five acres in size. Since few villagers own much more than one acre of land, Fawzia's father is fairly well-to-do.

In Egypt, farmers are called *fellahin,** the Arabic word for "those who plow the land." Like most fellahin, Ahmed and his family live in the village, not on the land they farm. Ahmed's house is one story high and has three rooms, built around a courtyard. The family of six lives in two of the rooms. The third serves as a kind of stable for the family's animals — a cow, a donkey, a water buffalo, and some chickens. Like most fellahin, Ahmed cannot afford a separate stable outside his house.

The house, like all the others, is made of mud brick. The floors are of beaten earth, pressed down until they are firm and level. The roof is flat, covered with palm boughs and straw. Except for the date palms which line the banks of the Nile, Egypt has few trees whose wood is hard enough to use for building. The date trees are too valuable to be cut down for wood. So from ancient times the people have built their homes of stone or of mud bricks mixed with straw and dried in the sun.

Life in the village begins each day with a prayer at dawn. In towns and villages, people are called to prayer by the muezzin, a man employed just for this purpose. Five times a day the muezzin climbs the stairs to the top of the minaret, the tower of the mosque, and calls out over the rooftops to the people. At dawn, his opening words include the reminder, "Prayer is better than sleep...."

Fawzia awakens each morning to this call. Everyone in the family — Fawzia; her parents; and her three brothers, Hashem,* 17, Hamid,* eight, and Fouad,* four — sleeps on cotton mattresses which are rolled up and stacked against the wall during the day. The room in which the family sleeps serves also as kitchen and dining room.

Fawzia's first task each morning is to milk the water buffalo. The members of her family always have fresh milk for breakfast, as well as tea and bread. Often they also have cheese and sometimes brown beans left to cook during the night. But the family does not eat the eggs their chickens lay; they save those to sell.

By the time the family finishes breakfast, the sun is well up and the village streets are crowded with people. Ahmed and Hashem trudge off to the fields. Hamid rushes off to school. And Fawzia goes to the village well. Many of the village girls will be doing the same, and she will meet most of her friends there.

With her water jar, Fawzia leaves the house, taking care to cover the lower part of her face with a veil of sheer black material. On her way to the well, Fawzia passes the road leading to the fields where Ahmed and Hashem are watering the land with a device known as a *shadoof.* * It consists of a long pole which swings up and down somewhat like a seesaw. A bucket, attached to one end of the pole, is pushed down into the water, then lifted and swung round — to tip its load into an irrigation ditch. To U.S. farmers this might seem a tedious way to water crops. But it works, and Egyptian farmers have used it for more than 3,000 years.

In fact, such devices are being used overtime these days, for farmers along the Nile generally do more planting than they used to. They are doing so largely because of dams built by the government in recent years. These dams store up much of the water from fall flooding, for irrigation use during the dry season. The biggest dam of all was completed in 1970 at Aswan,* a town in southern Egypt. Called the Aswan High Dam, it is one of the biggest in the world.

Before such dams were built, most Egyptian fellahin planted one crop a year — after the fall floods. Now that the dams provide water all year round, Ahmed and the men of his village now plant two crops. And in some parts of the country, the fellahin grow three crops a year.

After their long morning's work at the shadoof, Ahmed and Hashem are ready for an early lunch. Fawzia brings it to them in the fields at about 11 o'clock. After lunch, the men sleep through the early afternoon hours, the hottest part of the day. Then they work again until dusk.

Evenings are quiet in Fawzia's village. Supper is a hot meal, perhaps bean soup or stewed beans, or fish from the Nile. Every one or two months there may be some chicken or water buffalo, but most fellahin cannot afford meat more often than that. After supper Fawzia and her mother work in their home, while Ahmed goes to the coffeehouse. There he discusses village news with the other fellahin.

☆　☆　☆　☆　☆　☆　☆　☆　☆

Except for market day, an occasional wedding, or a celebration for the birth of a baby, Fawzia and her family rarely take a day off from work. Even if they

From the roof of his mosque in the Nile valley, a muezzin calls the people to prayer.

56

"Prayer is better than sleep...."

could afford to, they would have little reason. One day in the village is like another; nothing seems to change and few strangers ever appear. No wonder the villagers eagerly look forward to the few holidays when they can do something different.

The two biggest holidays of the Moslem year are known as the "Big Feast," and the "Little Feast." The Big Feast comes at the beginning of the ninth month of the Moslem calendar, and the Little Feast comes at the end of it. Moslems call this month *Ramadan.** It is holy to them because it was the month in which Allah began to reveal to Mohammed the words later collected in the Koran. For the entire month of Ramadan, Moslems fast during daylight hours.

Night is turned almost into day during Ramadan. From about 1 A.M. until an hour before dawn, the streets echo with the cries of a man who walks around town waking people and reminding them to eat while they can. The moment the first streak of light appears in the night sky, the fast will begin. The family cannot eat or drink again until sunset, when the fast is over for another night.

Aside from such holidays, Fawzia's days hardly change. But that does not bother her much. She is content to live out her life in her small, sunny village on the banks of the Nile. It is the only life she knows.

☆ ☆ ☆ ☆ ☆ ☆ ☆ ☆ ☆

In thousands of villages throughout the Arab world poor people live out their lives in much the same manner as Fawzia and her family. Of course, some of the villages look different. In North Africa, for example, olive groves and grape vineyards often cover the hillsides. Many North Africans depend on the vineyards for their living as much as Egyptians depend on growing grains and vegetables.

For the most part, though, the life of the Arab farmer is much the same in most areas of the Middle East. One village is much like another: the same cluster of small houses, a winding dirt street, and tiny shops. The men gather in the coffeehouse; the women meet at the well or the river's edge. In some countries — Lebanon, for example, or Kuwait — the children probably have a school to go to; in others they may not. Whether the farmers own or rent their land, their plots are always small — barely big enough for scratching out a living.

All Arab governments are training more teachers and building more schools. Many of them also have land reform programs. This means the farmers are given land of their own and taught modern farming methods. Irrigation projects — such as the construction of dams in Egypt to store the flood waters of the Nile — also help. But more time and more money are needed before these programs can have widespread results. Progress is very slow.

Fawzia will probably never leave her village. Neither will Hashem, her elder brother. His life may be somewhat easier than his father's. But he will always be a farmer who works hard to support his family.

If Hamid, the middle brother, could go on to a free public secondary school, new opportunities would then be open to him. But Hamid will probably not get past the village school, for there is no secondary school anywhere near his village. Ahmed always needs more help in the fields, and he will probably want Hamid to stay near home.

Fouad's future is a question mark. It depends on how much progress his country makes in the next several years. If Fouad and other young people like him can have the opportunity for an easier life, the Arab world may have met one of its greatest challenges.

Double-check

Review

1. Why do many Egyptian farm villages have high walls around the settlements?

2. Since ancient times, of what materials have the people of Egypt built their homes?

3. What is the duty of a muezzin?

4. What is Aswan, and why is this town important?

5. Why is the month of Ramadan holy to Moslems?

Discussion

1. Despite all its benefits, the Aswan Dam prevents silt from the upper Nile River from flowing south to enrich the farmlands of the lower Nile. Knowing its benefits and drawbacks, do you think the dam should have been built? Can you think of examples in the United States where such technological "improvements" caused environmental problems? Do you think these "improvements" should have been made? Who should make the final decisions in such situations? Explain your answers.

2. In 1952 the Egyptian government attempted to redistribute farmland from richer to poorer farmers. But today most Egyptian farmers are still poor and have small plots. Why do you suppose the government's attempt at land reform did not work? What aspects of Egyptian culture might influence farming methods?

3. Which person has a life more similar to your own — Fawzia of the Nile valley, or Hassan the Bedouin? Which one's life is most likely to change in the future? Is either person's life similar to the image you had of an Arab's life before you read these chapters? Explain your answers.

Activities

1. Some students might wish to draw a map of Egypt showing the Aswan Dam, Cairo, Alexandria, the Nile River, the Nile Delta, the Pyramids of Giza, Port Said, the Suez Canal, and Lake Nasser.

2. Several students could cooperate to assemble a scrapbook comparing farm products and tools of the Middle East and of the United States.

3. One student could play the part of Fawzia and pretend she is visiting the class. Others could interview "Fawzia" on how she feels about religion, education, the role of women, her role in her family, and her future.

Skills

WHEAT PRODUCTION IN EGYPT
1961–1975

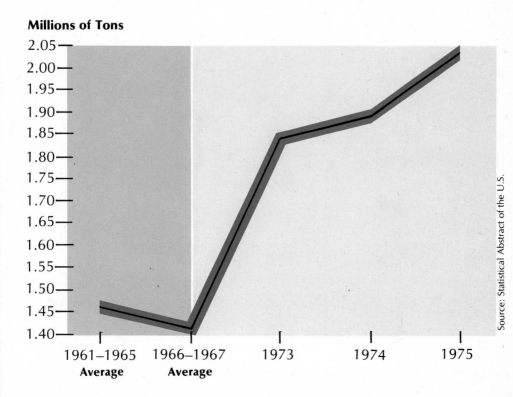

Millions of Tons

Source: Statistical Abstract of the U.S.

Use the line graph above and information in Chapter 4 to answer the following questions.

1. What do the numbers on the left of the graph represent?

2. What is the source of the information in this graph?

3. How many tons of wheat were produced in 1973?

4. During what two periods was there a decline in Egyptian wheat production?

5. During what period was there the greatest production increase? What project might help account for this increase?

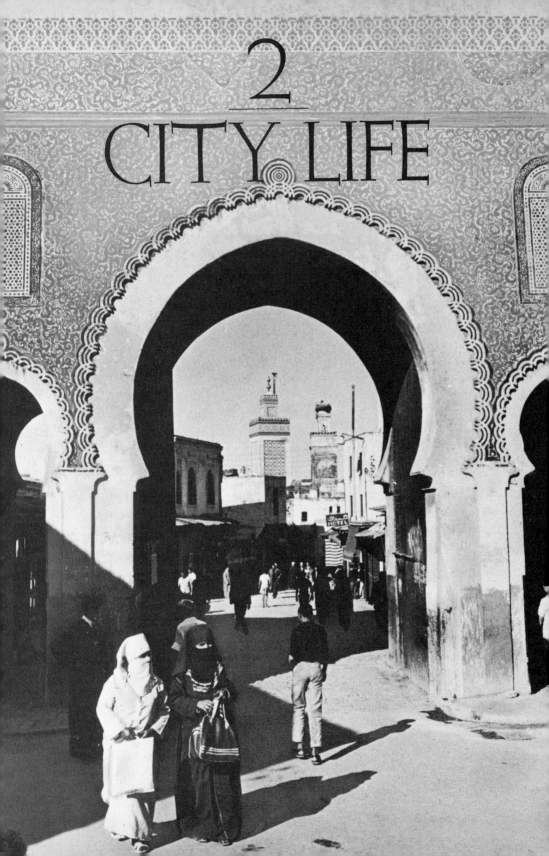

2
CITY LIFE

Chapter 5

Medinas and the Modern World

FOR THE MOST PART, Middle Easterners are not city people. Only about one in three Middle Easterners lives in or around cities. In some places — Saudi Arabia or Iran, for example — that proportion drops even lower. But in the nations of Israel and Kuwait, the majority of the people are city-dwellers. Eight of 10 Israelis live in or around cities.

Then why are Middle Eastern cities important?

Actually the cities have an importance far greater than the numbers of people living in them. It is in the cities that government, for the most part, is run. Cities provide the workers and the energy which move most Middle Eastern industries. They provide farmers with the large markets they need for selling their produce. In the cities, Middle Eastern music, art, architecture, and literature thrive. City universities turn out a yearly crop of graduates whose skills the region so badly needs. And it is in the cities that Middle Easterners have raised to a fine art one of their favorite occupations — trade.

Many of the cities of the Middle East have histories which date back more than a thousand years. Some of them, such as Damascus,* the capital of Syria, grew up at important points on the great trade routes. Others, such as Baghdad* in Iraq and Cairo in Egypt, grew up on the banks of great rivers. Wherever they sprouted, most of these cities were built with at least two main considerations in mind.

The first was religion. Reverence for Islam led to locating the mosque at the heart of the settlement. The second need was protection — especially from Bedouin tribesmen who had the unhappy habit of raiding the settlements from time to time in search of food. To protect against these raids, cities were often built on bluffs or other hard-to-reach places and were almost always enclosed by high walls.

Inside these walls most streets were little more than crooked alleys which twisted through the heart of the city like the paths in a labyrinth. Along these streets city-dwellers built homes designed for privacy. Most stood two or three stories high, and had no windows at the street level. Higher up, windows were closely shuttered or had carved wooden screens so that people inside could look out but no one outside could look in. Most homes had inside courtyards, many of which were planted with beautiful flowers and cooled by splashing fountains.

The grander these homes became, the greater were some cities' reputations for magnificence. Wealthy landowners often moved there, living off the rents or much of the harvest of the peasants who worked the land. In Egypt rulers known as sultans built palaces and gardens in the cities. Craftsmen and small shop-

In an Algerian market, each merchant tends
to be his own boss. What might be some
advantages to this system? some drawbacks?

keepers sold their handmade wares — precious jewelry, rich rugs and fabrics, pottery, and other objects — in the great city marketplaces, or *bazaars.*

The streets were as noisy as they were crowded. Loaded carts creaked, camels whined, and donkeys brayed. Horses, which only the rich could afford, added to the congestion. Street merchants called out, selling fruit drinks and food on every corner. Porters offered to carry people's bundles. Beggars continually asked for money, for the Koran commands Moslems to be charitable.

A Moslem wedding party, accompanied by musicians — or a funeral procession, with loudly weeping mourners — might pass by at any moment. Buyers and sellers bargained all day in the bazaars. And five times a day, louder than all the other sounds, came the call to prayer from the minarets of all the mosques in the city.

Today new sights and new sounds have been added to the old in the cities of the Middle East. The old quarters still exist, but only as part of newer, more modern cities. Usually the old quarter is known as the *medina,** the Arabic word for "city." Within the medinas, narrow streets still snake their way past windowless homes. Ancient bazaars still serve as an outlet for merchants selling their wares.

But new cities have grown up around the old. These new cities provide sights and sounds all their own. The whining of camels and the braying of donkeys can still be heard along some city thoroughfares. But now they are frequently drowned out by the rumble of jackhammers and the tootling horns of taxicabs.

Outside the medinas, wide avenues have replaced narrow, winding streets. Autos, buses, and bicycles have slowly eased donkey carts off the streets. Apart-

✑ To outsiders the slums are eyesores; to slum-dwellers they are graveyards of broken dreams.

ment buildings have taken the place of old, single-family homes. Hotels and office buildings have shot skyward in a Western-style salute to concrete and steel.

Around the outer rim of the downtown areas stretch the suburbs where many of those who work in the city live. Here, too, are slums — clusters of tumble-down shacks built from scraps of lumber, old tin cans, and similar materials. To outsiders the slums are eyesores; to slum-dwellers they are all-too-often graveyards of broken dreams.

Many slum-dwellers once lived as peasants in overcrowded villages. Blocked by lack of opportunity, they left their homes and came to the cities to be "in on things" — especially higher paying jobs in industry. Since they lacked industrial skills, however, many of them had to settle for low-paying jobs as household servants or day laborers. Over the years they have eked out an existence without much money and without the means of making more. By now many of them have found that city life is no better than life in the villages — that, in some ways, it is worse.

Their poverty stems partly from a problem which has plagued most of the Middle East for generations: that, except for Israel, the region lacks the industries to provide jobs for all those who want them.

One possible solution is to create more industries, and for decades these countries have been trying to do just that. But to build industry takes money and there are very few Middle Easterners who have enough of it to take chances on new industries. Those who do have money sometimes prefer to invest it elsewhere — in land, for example.

Countries without much oil income, such as Egypt, have to build the slow way. Countries with the vast new oil wealth — Iran, Saudi Arabia, and Kuwait, for example — have spent huge sums building new schools and industries.

Working hand in hand, the growth of industry and the spread of schools have brought about another change in Middle Eastern life. No longer are the cities the home of only two groups: the few very rich and the many very poor. In recent years these cities have also become the home of a growing number of doctors, lawyers, teachers, engineers, business people — all members of a rising middle class.

So, for all their many drawbacks, the cities still offer opportunities which are available nowhere else in the Arab world. As they continue to spread outward and upward, they produce the people and the goods which can help to make the region prosper.

NORTH AFRICA

For a knowledge of the stars, European scientists relied heavily on Arab astronomers, shown in this old European woodcut.

THE ARABS COME FORTH

LONG BEFORE the Arab-Israeli hostilities of the present day, another war in the Middle East made history. This war took place more than 1,300 years ago, but it, too, brought great changes to the area. This time the conquerors were Arabs.

The outside world then knew little about the Arabs. They came from a land few had seen, a place so blisteringly hot and forbiddingly dry that the great conquerors of the past — Babylonians,* Persians, Greeks, and Romans — had shunned it. Suddenly, about the year 633 A.D., the Arabs burst upon the world scene, leaving their mark throughout the Middle East and beyond.

Their armies were made up of Bedouin tribesmen who had roamed the deserts of Arabia in search of grass and water for their camels, horses, and goats. For centuries the Bedouins had fought among themselves. And for centu-

70

ries they had raided tribes living on the borders of Arabia and taken away their cattle.

It was Mohammed, with his new religion, who united the Arab tribes and organized them into armies. Between 622 and 632 A.D., thousands of Bedouins converted to the new faith. In adopting it, they also adopted one of its basic teachings — that Moslem must never fight Moslem. The more widely Islam took hold in Arabia, the farther afield Bedouin warriors had to go to find non-Moslem people to plunder.

In 633 they invaded Syria, an area which then included the present-day nations of Syria, Jordan, Lebanon, and Israel. The hard life of the Bedouins had toughened them and made them expert fighters; their new faith, Islam, molded them into fearless men with a mission. In Syria the Bedouins faced the troops of a great military power, the Byzantine* Empire. The Byzantines were far more numerous and far better armed than the Bedouins.

Yet the Arabs won the opening battles. Mounted on camels and horses, they charged furiously into the enemy lines again and again. Then in hand-to-hand combat they finished off their foes. Almost all of Syria, including the capital city of Damascus, fell to the Arabs.

One of the last cities to hold out was Jerusalem. To the Arabs, as to the Jews and Christians, Jerusalem was a holy city, for one of the most revered places of Islam was located there. Moslems believed that only a few years earlier Mohammed, astride a winged animal, had used a rock in Jerusalem as a steppingstone to ascend into heaven. To conquer the city and gain control of the rock now became an important Arab goal.

Slowly the Arabs tightened the knot, hemming in the city with their other conquests. In 638 Jerusalem finally fell. The man who accepted its surrender was an Arab leader named Omar,* whom Moslems called *caliph** (meaning the "successor" to Mohammed). He entered the city and hurried to pray at the sacred rock.

Those first victories in Syria proved only a beginning for the Arabs. During the next century they conquered Egypt and all of North Africa. Then they crossed the

Strait of Gibraltar* and conquered the Iberian Peninsula, today's Spain and Portugal. Their armies even pushed into southern France before they were defeated and turned back at the Battle of Tours in 732.

Nor did Arab warriors confine themselves only to the Middle East. They swept north through the lands now called Iran and Iraq, and east as far as India and the borders of China. Where Arab fighters did not go, Arab tradesmen often did. Over the course of several centuries, these tradesmen worked their way down the Malay Peninsula of Southeast Asia and onto the islands that now make up Indonesia and the Philippines.

Into every country they went, the Arabs took their language and religion. In time they spread Islam halfway around the globe from Morocco in the west to Indonesia in the east. They also spread the Arabic language across most of the Middle East (although other languages — Turkish, Persian, and Berber, for example — continued to prevail in large areas). The Middle East now became mainly an Arab domain.

The capital of this domain was the city of Baghdad. At Baghdad, between 750 and 850 A.D., Arab culture reached its most elaborate heights. That city gained fame for its wealth and splendor, as depicted in the tales of *The Arabian Nights.*

It also gained fame for its scholarship. At a time when Europe was sunk in the Dark Ages, Arab scholars were swapping ideas of a more advanced sort. In particular, they studied Indian mathematics and Greek medicine, geometry, and science. Arab scholars made one of their most important contributions by translating into Arabic the works of the ancient Greeks. When Europeans first "discovered" the works of Greek scientists hundreds of years later, they read those works in Arabic.

In the 13th century, the grandeur of the Arab world began to fade. Other conquerors came and left their mark on the Middle East. Baghdad fell to ruins as dusty as the nearby desert. In 1492 Arab armies were finally driven from Spain. But the accomplishments of the Arab empire at its height have lived on in memory and legend.

THE
ARAB EMPIRE
8th Century A.D.

→ Route of Expansion

PERSIA

ARABIAN
SEA

CASPIAN SEA

PERSIAN GULF

ARABIA

Tigris R.
Baghdad
Euphrates R.

SEA

RED

BLACK SEA

BYZANTINE EMPIRE

Damascus
Jerusalem

EGYPT

Nile River

MEDITERRANEAN
SEA

Danube River

BERBERS

IBERIAN
PENINSULA

Tours

Statute Miles

0   200   400   600   800   1000

N
W   E
S

Double-check

Review

1. About what fraction of Middle Easterners live in or around cities?

2. To protect against Bedouin raids, where were Middle Eastern cities often built?

3. What does the word *medina* mean in English?

4. What happened to the Arabs at the Battle of Tours in 732 A.D.?

5. What was the capital city of the Arab domain between 750 and 850 A.D.?

Discussion

1. Poverty, unemployment, and lack of good housing remain as major problems for cities of the Middle East. What efforts can these cities make to solve the problems? What efforts have U.S. cities — including your own — made to solve these problems? Do you think these problems can be solved? If so, how? If not, why not?

2. In a relatively short time, the Arabs were able to extend their empire from Spain to Indonesia. Why do you suppose the Arabs were so effective in spreading their religion and culture?

3. How do you suppose our lives might have been different if there never had been a great age of Arab civilization at the time when Europe was "sunk in the Dark Ages"?

Activities

1. Students who like to draw might make sketches of life in various cities of the Middle East. Others could research Middle Eastern architecture and draw public and private buildings. Some students could research and report on why their own city or other U.S. cities were founded where they were.

2. Some students might work together in constructing a timeline of Arab history from the birth of Mohammed to the year 1492. They should be sure to include on this timeline important dates and events mentioned in the chapter.

3. Other students might wish to research and write a report on contributions made by Arabs during the golden age of Arab civilization. Possible subjects could include astronomy, art, architecture, medicine, geometry, science, and literature.

Skills

POPULATION DENSITY OF SEVERAL MIDDLE EASTERN COUNTRIES

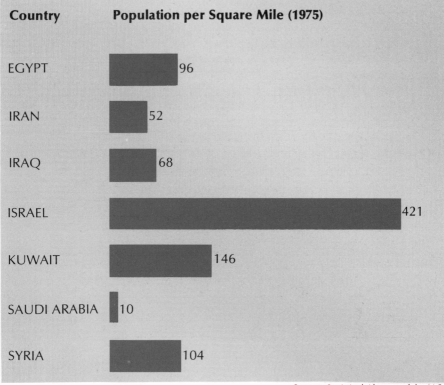

Country	Population per Square Mile (1975)
EGYPT	96
IRAN	52
IRAQ	68
ISRAEL	421
KUWAIT	146
SAUDI ARABIA	10
SYRIA	104

Source: Statistical Abstract of the U.S.

Use the bar graph above and information in Chapter 5 to answer the following questions.

1. What do the bars represent? For what year is the information given?

2. According to the graph, what does population density mean?

3. If all the people in Iraq were spread evenly across the land, how many people would be in any one square mile?

4. Which two Middle Eastern countries shown have the densest populations?

5. Do all those countries shown which have vast new oil wealth have high population density?

Chapter 6

Cairo: Citadel of Change

MUNIR,* 14, LIVES in Cairo, the largest city of Egypt. It is also the largest city in all Africa and the Middle East, and one of the most modern capitals in the world. Three hundred miles to the south, Fawzia and her family in the Nile valley live in much the same way as their ancestors did when Cairo was new a thousand years ago. But Munir's life differs even from the way his grandparents lived.

Munir and his sister, Safiya,* 12, live with their parents in a five-room apartment. Their apartment house sits on an island in the middle of the Nile, just where the river passes through the center of Cairo. The island is a little more than two miles long, less than a half mile wide, and has many modern apartment buildings.

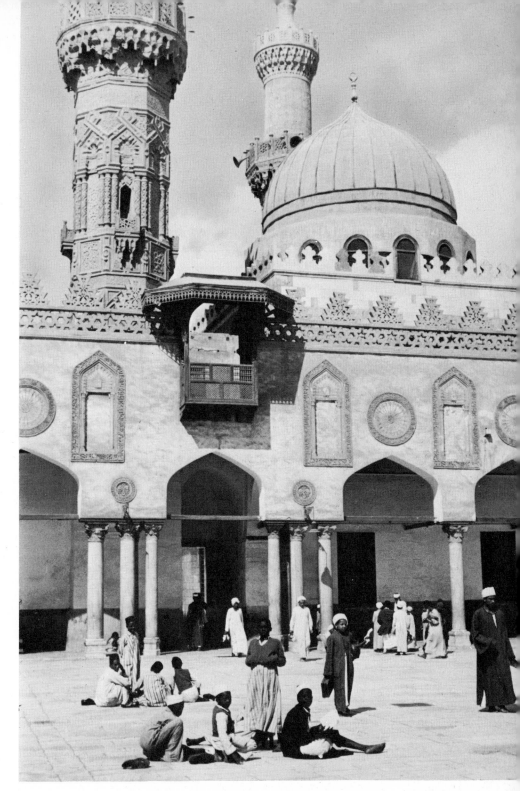

Moslem students and teachers at one of the world's oldest universities, al-Azhar in Cairo.

The apartment Munir lives in is like one in a Western country. Instead of floor cushions there are tables and chairs, and instead of sleeping mats, there are beds. The kitchen has running water, and an electric range and a refrigerator. In the living room is a television set. Munir and Safiya have their own radios.

In the morning, the calls of the muezzins from Cairo's many mosques boom over loudspeakers. The day begins later than it does in the rural areas of the Nile valley, but not as late as in a Western country. Schools and offices are already busy by seven or eight o'clock, so breakfast is early.

Munir eats breakfast in the dining room, on a chair at the table. He knows the old Arab way of eating. He has visited a village in the fertile Nile Delta, the farm area just north of Cairo, where his grandfather was a headman. There he has seen people eat with their fingers, everyone taking his food from a single dish. But Munir's family table is set as in Western countries, with knives, forks, and spoons.

In one way, though, Munir's breakfast is likely to be similar to Fawzia's — it very often includes brown beans. The beans are cooked in oil and well seasoned. But where Fawzia's family will sell any eggs its chickens lay, Munir's family often has eggs for breakfast.

Munir's father works for the Egyptian government. He is a farm expert and member of the department which helps fellahin to increase their crop production. Munir is in his third and last year in a preparatory school, which is like the ninth grade of a junior high school in the United States. He studies history, science, mathematics, the Koran, and English as well as Arabic. Next year he will begin three years of high school. Then he plans to enter Cairo University.

Munir thinks the Arabic he is studying is just as

difficult as a foreign language. This is because it is the written "classical" Arabic of the Koran. It differs from the ordinary spoken Arabic that Munir and his family speak. For Munir, learning classical Arabic is somewhat like an American student learning to speak the English that was spoken in England hundreds of years ago.

Safiya is still in elementary school. Her school is co-ed, but next year, when she begins the preparatory course, she will go to a girls' school. In all Egyptian preparatory and high schools, girls and boys study separately.

Munir and Safiya travel to school by bus. Their section of Cairo is the newest part of the city. Most of the people there wear Western-style clothes, as do Munir and his family. Safiya is dressed in her school uniform — blouse, skirt, and jacket. Munir wears a dark suit.

Now and then Munir sees someone in the crowd wearing the traditional robes of the Egyptian villagers. A man selling cold Pepsi-Cola at an umbrella-covered street stand is dressed this way. But his costume looks old-fashioned next to the new banks, department stores, and office buildings in this part of town.

Far across the city to the east is the Citadel, or fortress, built 800 years ago. There things look quite different. Students can be seen on their way to one of the oldest educational institutions in the world, al-Azhar* University. Al-Azhar was founded a thousand years ago by the Arab conquerors in Egypt. Although many new buildings have been added, the oldest one, the mosque of al-Azhar, is still the center of the university. At al-Azhar many classes are held in the old mosque itself. There the students sit on rugs on the ground, grouped around their teacher.

Schools, offices, and shops in large Egyptian cities such as Cairo close early in the afternoon. Work usually stops by two o'clock, and people start home for a leisurely lunch and a long rest. The hottest hours of the day are in the early afternoon, and everyone wants to be indoors and out of the sun. Businessmen usually start back to work about four o'clock and stay at their desks or tend their shops until about eight in the evening.

In the villages girls and boys, unless they belong to the same family, are usually kept apart before marriage. This isn't usually true any more in Cairo or other large Egyptian cities. Some of the school clubs to which Munir and Safiya belong include both boys and girls. But neither Munir nor Safiya goes out on dates alone.

Safiya knows that most Egyptian parents pick out husbands for their daughters. She vows that, when the time comes, she is going to choose her husband for herself. But first she wants to go to Cairo University.

The family has dinner, the main meal of the day, together at home. Moslems do not eat pork, but they eat a great deal of lamb and chicken. Pigeon and fish are popular, too. Since the villagers keep their cows as work animals, there is not much beef. Most often, Munir and his family have lamb for dinner. Munir's mother serves this as *kebab** — bite-size pieces flavored with garlic and cooked on skewers. With it there are vegetables and a salad, and for dessert, fruit — perhaps watermelon or cantaloupe — or pastry. Arab pastry is sweet and rich, made with sugar, butter, almonds or pine nuts, and much honey. With dinner the family drinks strong tea or coffee.

Then comes the best time for enjoying oneself in Cairo — the long evening. People tend to stay up late in Egyptian cities. They have had a long rest in the afternoon, and they like to take advantage of the cool nights.

Neither Safiya nor her mother goes out alone in the evenings, but the family may go out together. Sometimes they go to a play or a concert, and sometimes just to the movies. These family outings often take place on Thursday nights, which are like Saturday nights in the U.S. Friday is the Moslem day of rest, just as Saturday is the Jewish day of rest and Sunday the Christian day of rest.

On some Thursday nights the family joins the strollers along the tree-lined streets. People buy fruit drinks and roasted corn-on-the-cob from street vendors. Little boats with tall sails glide up and down the Nile, taking people on tours of the river.

Munir thinks his city is beautiful at night, but most beautiful during the nights of Ramadan. All day long many people have fasted, and at sundown they are ready to enjoy themselves. Restaurants and cafes bustle with activity until dawn. Shops do not close, and theaters have late shows. Music and merrymaking are everywhere.

In the midst of the gaiety, people do not forget to pray. Crowds flock to the mosques, kept open all night during this month. The minarets are lighted and their reflection sparkles on the Nile. At this time of year two Cairos are on view — the new and modern one where Munir lives, and the old and fabled one where the sultans ruled, surrounded by "all the delights of this life."

Double-check

Review

1. By what time in the morning are schools and offices in Cairo busy?

2. When, and by whom, was al-Azhar University founded?

3. What are the meats that Munir and his family eat most often?

4. Why do people tend to stay up late in Egyptian cities?

5. What day is the Moslem day of rest?

Discussion

1. Compare life in the three different places you have studied so far: Hassan's "house of hair" tent, Fawzia's mud brick house, and Munir's city apartment. How do these dwellings compare with the one in which you live? In which of them would you most like to live? Least like to live? Why?

2. In what ways is Munir's life similar to Fawzia's? In what ways are their lives different? Do you think that growing up in the countryside or in a city makes any difference in the type of career that Egyptian — or American — young people choose? Should it make a difference?

3. In Cairo, people arise early and stay up late, but they rest in the afternoon. For what reasons do they schedule their days this way? Why do you schedule your day the way you do? How is it different from a typical Egyptian's day? Which do you prefer? Why?

Activities

1. Some students could pretend they are tourists in Cairo and write a travel diary about the differences they notice between life in Cairo and life in their own city or town. Some of the "tourists" could write about visiting Cairo during the month of Ramadan.

2. A committee of students might watch television and read newspapers and magazines for reports of current events in Cairo. Articles, photos, and political cartoons could be displayed on a bulletin board under appropriate headings.

3. Several students could research why and when Cairo was founded, how the city is laid out, what historic events have happened there, and what famous buildings and gardens Cairo has. Then they could make an oral report to the class.

Skills

TYPES OF COMMUNICATIONS IN THE MIDDLE EAST

Country	Telephones in Use**	Daily Newspaper Circulation**	Radios in Use*	Television Sets in Use*
EGYPT	503	773	5,115	610
IRAN	688	484	8,000	1,500
ISRAEL	813	1,330	680	441
MOROCCO	168	235	1,300	382
SAUDI ARABIA	85	96	85	122
TURKEY	1,012	(NA)	4,096	458
(all numbers in thousands)				

* 1974 Figures
** 1975 Figures
NA — Not Available

Source: Statistical Abstract of the U.S.

Use the table above and information in Chapter 6 to answer the following questions.

1. What do the numbers in the table stand for?

2. What does the symbol (*) stand for? What does (NA) stand for?

3. How many television sets were in use in Morocco in 1974?

4. In what category is it impossible to tell which country ranks first or last?

5. Is the largest city in the Middle East located in a country that has the greatest number of radios?

Chapter 7

Fez: The Tread of the Past

IN SOME WAYS Munir has quite a bit in common with another Arab teenager, Khaled.* Both are Moslems, and both are the same age, 14. Like Munir, Khaled lives in an Arab country, Morocco. Like Munir, Khaled lives in a city, Fez. But the similarities stop there, for Khaled's life is very different from Munir's.

Parts of Fez are as modern as the part of Cairo in which Munir lives. For about 50 years, until 1956, the French ruled Morocco. In Fez they built wide, tree-lined avenues and Western-style houses, hotels, and office buildings. But the part of Fez in which Khaled lives is the oldest section, the medina, and it is separated from the newer city by an ancient wall.

The old town is almost 1,200 years old. About the year 800 the first Arab ruler of Morocco, a great-grandson of Mohammed, founded Fez. The narrow streets are either dirt or paved with cobblestones. Because the old town is built on a hillside most of the streets slope steeply. Some have steps built into them. Most homes have no windows at all facing on the street.

Just outside the medina walls, buses speed by on the modern streets of the newer city. Inside there is no room even for automobiles. Instead, donkeys and bicycles jam the lanes.

Khaled's family has lived in the medina for generations. The men in the family have always earned their living as leather toolers, making delicate designs by hand on leather goods such as bookcovers, briefcases, and belts. Many of the designs are made in 18-carat gold. Fez is well known for fine leather and for the kind of leather work which Khaled's family does.

Khaled's father, Haroun,* inherited his leather tools from his father, who taught Haroun his craft. Khaled's older brother, Syed,* who is 25, learned from Haroun, and now Khaled is learning, too. In Khaled's family, fathers have always taught their sons the family trade.

Haroun's shop is in the bazaar area of the old town. Shops which sell similar kinds of goods are grouped together on the the same street in the bazaar. Haroun's shop is on the Street of the Leather Workers. There is also the Street of the Leather Makers, where Haroun buys the leather he uses in his work.

On the Street of the Coppersmiths, gleaming bowls, pitchers, and cups are hammered into shape by hand. Along the Street of the Dyers, bright skeins of red and yellow wool hang overhead, newly dyed and drying, later to be woven into rugs. On the Street of the Potters, the shops contain shelf after shelf of beautiful jars and vases in many shapes and colors — deep aquamarine, or designs of blue, yellow, red, and white. Along other streets merchants sell spices, perfumes, objects of brass, fabrics, gold and silver jewelry, and embroidery. They also sell prayer rugs, small carpets which many Moslems kneel on when they pray.

⏤ Along the Street of the Dyers, bright skeins of wool hang overhead, later to be woven into rugs.

Like the other shops, Haroun's is small and has an open front. It holds his work bench and a few shelves to display his goods, with little space for anything else. Some shops are even smaller — where some of the cloth-weavers sit working, the ceilings are so low that it is impossible to stand up.

Nearby is the home of Khaled's family. The house is made of stone, covered with whitewashed cement. It is one story high and has five large rooms. There is a courtyard in the center on which all the rooms open. Khaled, his parents, and his two sisters and younger brother live in two of the rooms, and his older brother Syed and Syed's wife and two young children live in the other two. The fifth room is the kitchen, which both families share.

From the outside most houses in the medina look alike. But inside they may be quite different. The homes of the rich have beautiful fountains and large gardens in their courtyards. The floors and walls of their many rooms are covered with beautiful painted tiles, and tables and chests are hand-carved. But most poor families live in houses of one or two rooms with little furniture or decoration.

Khaled and his family eat in traditional Arab style, sitting on the floor around a low, round table. With every meal they drink the most popular beverage in Morocco, mint tea. Moroccans take great care in making and serving tea, just as the Bedouins do with their coffee. Fresh mint leaves and tea leaves are placed in a silver or copper teapot, and boiling water

Dyed wool dries along Street of Dyers in Marrakesh, Morocco.

and a great deal of sugar are added. The tea is served in tiny glasses.

Khaled and his brother both attend public elementary school. Since Morocco became independent of France in 1956, all children are required by law to go to elementary school. Khaled is in his last year. His sisters went to school, too, although the oldest one went for only a few years. When she was younger, not enough schools had yet been built in Morocco, and many children could not attend at all. Many children still don't. Except in cities such as Fez, there still aren't enough schools.

Khaled studies most of the same subjects as Munir does, but he studies in two languages, French and Arabic. He is taught mathematics and science in French, and history and geography in Arabic. Most Moroccans speak French as well as Arabic, having learned it during the time of French rule.

Sometimes Khaled hears a third language. This is Berber, the language of the people who lived in Morocco and elsewhere in North Africa before the Arabs came. Many modern Moroccans are descendants of both Berbers and Arabs.

Other Moroccans who live in the countryside and the mountain villages have very little Arab blood. This is especially true of the people of the Rif hills of northern Morocco and of the Atlas Mountains which cut through the central and southern parts of the country. At the time of the Arab invasions, these people kept to themselves and did not mix with the Arabs. They still speak the old Berber language and follow many of the old Berber customs. Berbers, for example, never marry their first cousins, as the Arabs sometimes do. Even though the Berbers became Moslems, Berber women, when among their fellow Berbers, never wear veils.

In a region lacking fertile land for farming, Middle Easterners long ago became experts in another occupation — trade. This alert Arab merchant makes his living by selling grain.

In his free time Khaled likes to go to the movies, where many of the films are French or Egyptian. He and his friends like to play soccer. Sometimes he listens to popular music from the Western countries, especially the United States and France.

Khaled's sisters spend most of their time at home with their mother. They like the movies as much as Khaled does, but they never go to such public places unless their father or one of their brothers takes them. Outdoors they usually wear veils.

Haroun will probably choose husbands for his daughters soon, although they often joke about picking out their own. Haroun says "maybe," but they will have to be boys well known to the family — relatives or the sons of close friends. Haroun believes the old way of doing things is still the best way for his daughters.

Sometimes Khaled thinks about planning a life different from the old way. Once he wanted to learn all about his father's work and to join Haroun and Syed in the shop. Now he knows that there are many other things he might do for a living.

Haroun is proud of his two sons in school. When he was young, the only book to be studied was the Koran. In studying the Koran, students learned to read and write. Thus they were better off than most children who only learned to memorize verses from the Koran. Now Haroun doesn't seem to mind when Khaled talks about new ways of doing things. He does not mind when Khaled says he does not want to become a leather worker like Haroun.

Haroun knows that few of the old handcrafts are left. Much of what is sold in the bazaar now is machine-made. There are very few customers for hand-tooled leather and handmade rugs and pottery — most of the customers are tourists. Many Moroccans buy the new factory-made goods, which cost much less. In 20 years — or perhaps in only 10 or five — there may not be much of a living to be made from leather work.

Haroun would like to see Khaled leave the medina and go out into the newer city to live another kind of life. Khaled's education is giving him the chance to do this.

Double-check

Review

1. About when and by whom was the city of Fez founded?

2. What is the most popular beverage in Morocco?

3. Berber is the language of what people?

4. What mountain range cuts through central and southern Morocco?

5. When Haroun was young, what book did he study?

Discussion

1. Morocco was a French colony for many decades. How do you suppose that being a French colony has influenced the kind of country Morocco is today? Do you think that being a French colony has made Morocco different from Egypt or Saudi Arabia, and similar to Algeria (which was also a French colony)? How has the United States been influenced by being a former English colony? Explain your answers.

2. How can getting an education help Khaled live a life different from that of his father? What might Khaled do for a living if he decides to move to the newer city? Do you think that Khaled should become a leather worker like his father? If you were Khaled, would you want to move to the newer city? Explain your answers.

3. In the United States, there has been increased interest in handcrafts in recent decades. Why do you suppose this is so? Do you think handcrafts in Morocco will again become more popular and profitable? Why, or why not?

Activities

1. Some students might research and write reports on aspects of the history or government of Morocco.

2. Other students might create a bulletin board display titled "Life in Modern Morocco." Students could display pictures of the people, crafts, costumes, buildings, terrain, foods, and other aspects of life in Morocco today.

3. Some students might learn about one of the crafts mentioned in the chapter and give reports or demonstrations on the craft. Students could compare artistic styles in the Middle East and the United States in these crafts.

Skills

USING AN INDEX

Use the above listings from the index to this book and information in Chapter 7 to answer the following questions.

1. In what order are topics listed in an index?
　(a) by importance　(b) by page number　(c) alphabetically

2. On what page would you find an illustration of a muezzin?
　(a) 57　(b) 78　(c) 33

3. On how many pages in this text are mosques discussed?
　(a) 29　(b) two　(c) three

4. On what page is the first mention of Morocco?
　(a) 18　(b) 14　(c) 84

5. Which of the following subtopics shown on this index page describes the subject matter of Chapter 7?
　(a) life in Fez　(b) Moses　(c) mosques

Chapter 8

Teheran: Nightingales and Revolution

CONTRASTS ABOUND THROUGHOUT the Middle East, but in Teheran,* the capital of Iran, they are especially sharp. Teheran is a dizzying mixture of the old and the new. It is a metropolis of glass-walled skyscrapers, blinking neon lights, and traffic-clogged streets. Iranian motorists tend to drive with a carefree attitude, and are noted more for their skill in steering around obstacles than for their care or courtesy.

Yet along these same streets walk Iranian women draped in huge scarflike coverings. Though the requirement that women be veiled in public was abolished in 1935, the renewal of Islamic fervor in 1979 brought the return of veils to most women in public. A walk through the Great Bazaar of Teheran is like a walk into the past. Here the 20th century melts into the old Orient. The bazaar is a fragrant patchwork of colors, spices, fruits, nuts, rugs, and fabrics.

Yasmine,* who lives in Teheran, is a Moslem but she is not an Arab. Iran is not an Arab country. Most of the people trace their heritage back to the Aryans, a people who moved into the region 4,000 years ago. The name *Iran* means "land of the Aryans." The Greeks called the land "Persia," and this name stuck in the West. But Iranians have always called their homeland "Iran." Arab Moslems conquered the land in the seventh century, and since then Islam has been the religion of the Iranian people.

Yasmine lives in an elegant apartment on the north side of Teheran. The apartment's floors are covered with deeply colored Persian rugs woven to ancient patterns. Because she is female, Yasmine has never been inside one of Teheran's most unusual places, a *zurkhaneh,** or house of strength. The houses of strength date so far back in time that no one knows exactly how they started. They are a kind of cross between a gym and a secret lodge.

Men who arrive at the zurkhaneh in modern business suits change into baggy knee-length trousers. Then they participate in a bare-chested ritual workout in a pit. Drums beat, and the master chants a 10th-century epic poem. The men begin to swing enormous clubs. The drums beat faster, and the men leap, spin, and juggle the heavy clubs until they are exhausted.

After the ritual, they shower, put their business suits back on, and disappear into office buildings. There is something about this practice that is very much in character with Iran. Iranians are fiercely proud of their long, distinguished history.

Once a week, Yasmine and her family visit her grandparents in an old walled house in another part of town. Yasmine loves the tiny gardens at the house and the songs of the nightingales her grandmother keeps. Once a familiar tradition in Iranian life, nightingales

*A world apart from the glitter of the cities,
life in Iran's villages moves to a slower beat.
Above, a group of farmers gather by the mud-
baked walls of their village to exchange news.*

are disappearing. Today few people seem to have time to care for such fragile birds.

In recent years, much else has changed in the lives of Yasmine's grandparents. Her grandmother came from what was one of Iran's richest and most powerful old families. Once they owned large tracts of land in the northern part of the country. Like many members of Iran's nobility, they seldom visited their lands. Their agents collected the large rents from the peasants who farmed the land. It was customary to divide harvests under a "five-fifths" system. The crop was divided into five shares — one each for the persons supplying the land, water, seed, equipment, and labor. Since the landlord usually supplied the first four, he got four fifths of the harvest. The farmer, who supplied only the labor, ended up with just one fifth. The result of this system was that the largest portion of Iran's population was desperately poor and was tied to the land almost like serfs.

For years Iran's ruler, Shah Mohammed Riza Pahlevi,* tried to reform this pattern of land-holding. But the pace was very slow. Few landowners willingly gave up such easy income, even though the Iranian government offered to buy out the wealthy landowners. But Yasmine's grandparents accepted the offer in 1972. They put the money from the sale in real estate investments, especially in Teheran. As Iran's economy boomed, these investments became very valuable.

Iran's economic boom resulted mainly from the vast amount of money coming into the country through the sale of oil. Iran sits on top of about 10 per cent of the world's known oil reserves. And before 1979, Iran was the world's second largest exporter of oil (behind Saudi Arabia). This wealth drew into Teheran investors from all over the world and led to a tremendous building boom in the city.

The boom in Iran was interrupted in early 1979 by a political and social revolution that forced the shah out of power and out of the country. Iran's Moslem religious leaders seized control. The leader of the revolution was Ayatollah Ruhollah Khomeini.* He charged that the shah had tortured and killed thousands of Iranians during his reign. Khomeini also criticized the modernization that had taken place under the shah, and he tried to revive many ancient Moslem traditions.

Women were told to wear the long, black robes and veils that had been discouraged in the shah's reign. Many women did. Khomeini also looked for ways to combat foreign influence in Iran, especially Western influence. Strict censorship was imposed on newspapers, radio and television stations, books, and even music. Factories closed, building stopped, and oil production declined.

Then in November 1979, a large group of Iranians stormed the United States Embassy in Teheran and seized Americans as hostages. The Iranians demanded that the shah, who was receiving medical treatment in New York City, be returned to Iran for "trial and punishment." When the demand was refused, the hostages were held prisoners, despite almost worldwide condemnation of the action.

The shah voluntarily left the U.S. in December 1979 and died seven months later in Egypt. But the American hostages were not released until January 20, 1981. These events isolated Iran from most other nations of the world, even other Moslem nations.

Double-check

Review

1. What is the capital city of Iran?

2. What does the name *Iran* mean in English?

3. Since what event has Islam been the religion of the Iranians?

4. About what percentage of the world's oil reserves does Iran have?

5. What event in 1979 caused the shah to lose power and flee the country?

Discussion

1. When the Ayatollah Khomeini came to power in Iran, many women went back to wearing veils, and job opportunities for women lessened. Why do you think these changes were made? How might you have felt about these changes if you were a woman in Iran at the time? What, if anything, do these changes say about Iranian women's political power?

2. Do you think the "five-fifths" system of dividing harvests was fair to farmers? Why, or why not? How do you think the system arose? Why do you think the farmers accepted it for so many years? How was the "five-fifths" system similar to, and different from, the sharecropping system used in the United States?

3. How would you feel toward the new regime in Iran if you were Yasmine or her grandparents? What people in Iran supported the revolution? Do you think the revolution has benefited people in Iran? Explain your answers.

Activities

1. Some students might create a map of Iran which depicts its mountain ranges, rivers, cities, major bodies of water, and major oil fields.

2. Iran is famous for its hand-woven "Persian" carpets. Some students might bring pictures of these carpets to school. Other students could research and report to the class on how these carpets are made and designed.

3. Students might role-play a debate between the shah and the ayatollah on the subject "Modernization Is Good for Iran."

Skills

THE AYATOLLAH KHOMEINI SPEAKS

In Islam we want to implement a policy to purify society, and in order to achieve this aim, we must punish those who bring evil to our youth. Don't you do the same? When a thief is a thief, don't you throw him in jail? In many countries, don't you even execute murderers? Don't you use that system because, if they were to remain free and alive, they would contaminate others and spread their stain of wickedness?

— interview with Western journalist, 1979

Use the passage above and information in Chapter 8 to answer the following questions.

1. Under what circumstances did Khomeini say these words?
(a) in a speech   (b) in an interview   (c) on a radio show

2. What is the main topic of this passage?
(a) punishment of criminals   (b) Iranian youth   (c) jails

3. When Khomeini uses "you," whom does he mean?
(a) the journalist   (b) the Western world   (c) criminals

4. According to the passage, how should criminals be treated?
(a) turned free   (b) rehabilitated   (c) punished

5. Who is the Ayatollah Khomeini?

THE LAND

*As landscapes go, the Middle East is
marked by contrasts. There are forests
and mountains. Nature has also given the
region spectacular, unbroken horizons,
widest of all in the great Sahara (left)
and along the Mediterranean Sea (below).*

WATER: From the scrubby highlands of Turkey (far right) to the desert plains of Egypt (lower right), water is the lifeblood of the Middle East. For water, farmers rely on rivers such as the Jordan (below). But even some rivers go dry (right), and farmers must irrigate.

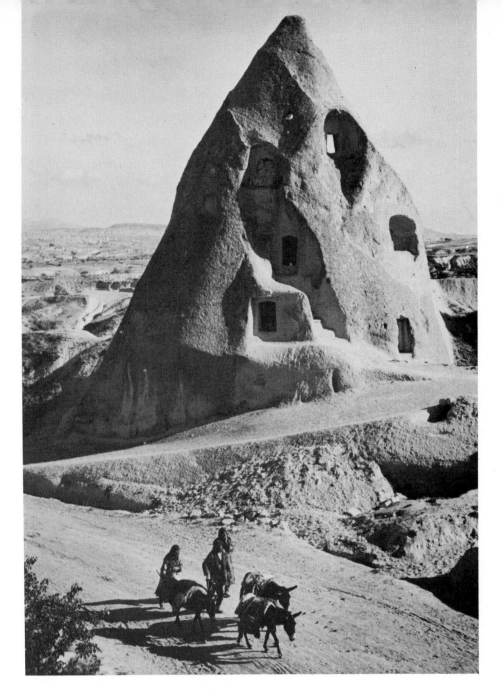

STRUCTURES: *Many Middle Eastern structures seem to spring from their natural surroundings — and some actually do. Top left, Roman ruins in Jordan. Bottom left, 1,200-year-old city of Shibbam in Saudi Arabian desert. Above, Turkish cave-dweller's home hewn from volcanic debris.*

HOMES: *Many Arabs dwell in cities such as Cairo (below). A handful of the wealthiest live in ornate palaces (above). But the vast majority of Middle Easterners live in dusty villages such as the one in Morocco pictured at left.*

THE
PEOPLE

Like people everywhere, Middle Easterners look forward to the small joys that make a life of hard work more bearable. Those joys may include a leisurely spin on the family hay wagon (left) or the chance to watch in wonder while the local magician runs through his list of tricks (below).

FACES: Lost in thought, locked in alarm, or lined with curiosity, Middle Eastern faces are a mosaic of attitudes and features. Left, Nile Valley peasants. Above, a Bedouin woman in Jordan. Right, cafe patrons in the city of Fez, Morocco.

AT EASE: Middle Easterners get special pleasure from the things they do with family or friends — whether it be a coffee break among elderly Turks (left), a baby-ogling lunch break in Israel (bottom left), or a family dinner in Tunisia (below). But even super-social people sometimes stray off into their own worlds like the Egyptian at right.

URBAN TEENS: Some Middle Eastern city-dwellers may have more in common with other people in distant cities than with villagers much nearer home. What similarities and differences do these photos reveal about young people in Tel Aviv (top left), Cairo (bottom left), and Beirut (above)?

THE
ECONOMY

"We are still struggling to bring our countries into the 20th century," says one Arab official. Part of the answer is trade, which now links past and present in a variety of ways. The past lingers in ancient bazaars such as the one in Tunis (left). The present pops up amid oil pipelines which cover Kuwait City docks (below).

FOOD: Where much of the land is lifeless,
people prize whatever food and livestock they
have. Moroccan shepherds inspect goats (above).
Iraqi fisherman prepares to cast a net into
the historic Tigris River (top right). Egyptian
fellahin women sort out corn (bottom right).

CLOTHING: Textiles are a major thread in the expanding loom of Middle Eastern industry. An Iranian woman checks spindles for making burlap (above). An Israeli designer creates textile patterns (top right). Egyptians sew clothes by hand (bottom right).

INDUSTRIES: Mines and machinery are useless without men to run them, and such men are in short supply in parts of the Middle East. Some who do exist: Israeli phosphate miners (top left), a Saudi oil refinery mechanic (bottom left), and a Libyan explosives expert (below).

THE CULTURE

"Your religions can spring up only on dry land, very dry land, all rocks and pits and sand deserts and burning sun, except for an occasional terrific thunderstorm from nowhere," said U.S. writer George Santayana. Do you agree? How might sun and sand and thunderstorms affect religious beliefs?

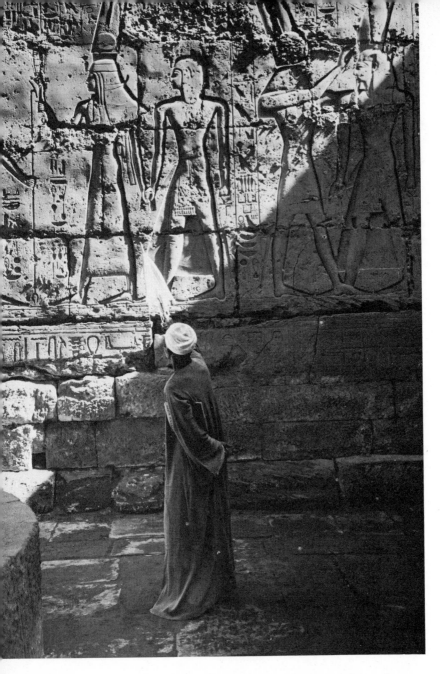

TRADITIONS: The Middle East has a special sense of history, for it was here that history began. Above, ancient temple carving in Luxor, Egypt. Top right, timeless craft of jewelry-making. Top far right, page from Moslem holy book, the Koran. Bottom right, Egyptians at cemetery near Giza pyramids.

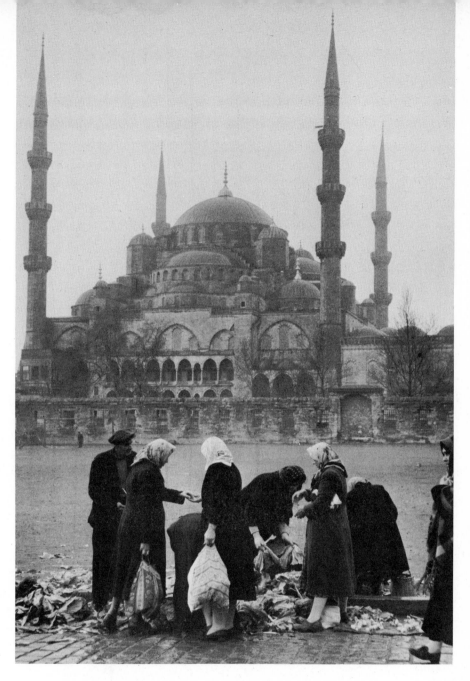

RELIGIONS: *As the birthplace of three major religions, the Middle East contains many impressive houses of worship, like Istanbul's Hagia Sophia mosque (above). But Middle Easterners also worship in simple surroundings. In Jerusalem a Moslem prays in street as son waits (top left), while Jews gather to pray at ancient Wailing Wall.*

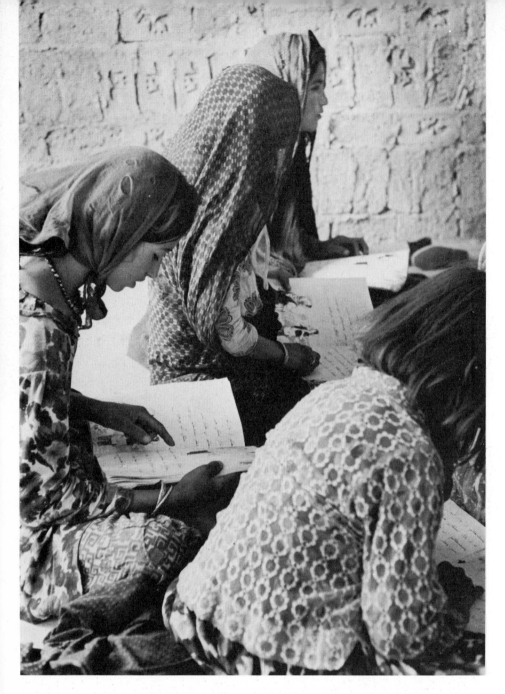

LEARNING: In the past few years, the chances for young Middle Easterners to get an education have expanded greatly. Above, Iranian women learn to read. Top right, children in a Cairo nursery. Right, Israeli students in the library at Jerusalem's Hebrew University.

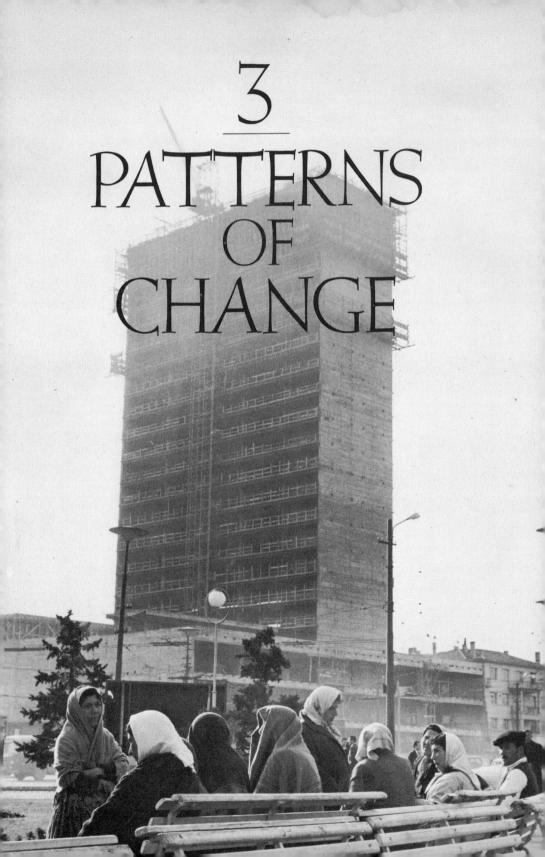

3
PATTERNS
OF
CHANGE

Turkey:
Astride Two Continents

AN ENGLISHMAN traveling in Turkey recently chose a train seat next to a group of Turkish soldiers. Part way through the trip, the soldiers began to heckle him about his homeland. Thinking this was good sport, the Englishman looked out the window, pointed to a loaded donkey near the tracks, and joked: "Turkish Cadillac!" The smiles disappeared from the faces of the Turkish soldiers. In a fit of anger, they pounced on the Englishman and beat him up.

As the Englishman later realized, he had injured the soldiers' sense of pride. By lashing out with their fists, the soldiers were telling him that they were proud to be Turks and they were not going to allow their country to be made the object of any jokes.

Over the course of many years, this sort of national spirit has become a Turkish trademark. In part, it is a pride in the things which make Turkey different from its neighbors. To be sure, the Turks do share some things in common with other Middle Easterners, especially their Moslem faith. Nonetheless, Turkey has its own geography, its own history, and its own language. All this sets the Turks apart from the other Moslem people of the Middle East.

One difference is visible on a map of the Middle East. Turkey is located both in Asia and in Europe. Slicing through the country is a waterway called the Turkish Straits (made up of the Bosporus,* the Sea of Marmara,* and the Dardanelles*). The straits also divide Europe from Asia, leaving Turkey with one foot in the East and just a big toe in the West.

The "big toe" is Turkish Thrace, a spit of land about the size of Massachusetts. Though this area contains the city of Edirne and part of Istanbul,* it is otherwise sparsely populated. The "foot" is Asian Turkey, which the ancient Greeks called Asia Minor and which today is called Anatolia. Shaped roughly like a rectangle, Anatolia is 32 times larger than Turkish Thrace in area and holds 90 per cent of the Turkish population.

Because of its continent-straddling position, Turkey serves as one of the most valuable pieces of real estate anywhere on the globe. It has long been used as a "funnel" through which armies have passed between the two continents. For centuries it also played host to a wide array of peoples who wandered there from all directions. They settled the area in a long series of migrations, which piled one cultural layer on top of another like tiers in a wedding cake.

The first known conquerors of the area were the Hittites, warlike peoples who swept into Asia Minor from central Asia about 3000 B.C. Over the centuries, others followed, including the Greeks and Romans who built settlements along the coast. The Greeks built magnificent temples whose ruins still stand to-

THE
OTTOMAN
EMPIRE
17th Century A.D.

Statute Miles
0   200   400   600   800   1000

ARABIAN
SEA

CASPIAN SEA

PERSIAN GULF

Tigris R.   Baghdad

Euphrates R.

Mecca

RED SEA

BLACK SEA

Cairo

Nile River

MEDITERRANEAN SEA

AEGEAN
SEA

Constantinople

Danube River

Vienna

Tripoli

N
W   E
S

day. The Romans used the coast as a sort of playpen, a place where the wealthy could cavort in the sun. The Roman Emperor Constantine made the city of Byzantium the capital of the entire Roman Empire in 330 A.D. — renaming it Constantinople. (Later the city would be renamed Istanbul by the Turks.)

But the area's most important migration still lay ahead. It began about the seventh and eighth centuries A.D., when Turkish peoples from East Asia started moving west. Along the way these peoples were converted to the new faith of Islam. In the 11th century they arrived in Anatolia and put down roots.

In their adopted homeland, the Turks built a fearsome reputation as fighters. After centuries of fighting among the various Turkish tribes, one tribe, the Ottomans, was clearly the most powerful. By the 15th century, the Ottomans had created their own empire, which stretched across much of the Middle East.

They owed their success as empire-builders to several things. One was the religious zeal shown by Moslem warriors in extending the kingdom of Allah. Another was the development of a skilled corps of shock troops once made up of former prisoners of war. A third was the Ottoman knack of making neighboring peoples feel at home in the empire once they had been conquered. All in all, the Ottomans were among the shrewdest rulers the world had ever seen.

In 1453 they seized the city of Constantinople and made it their capital. Then they went about building one of the most elaborate palaces ever designed anywhere. Known as Topkapi,* this palace had 400 rooms lined with marble floors and decorated with trappings such as golden water faucets. Amid this

Turkey has been called a nation poised between past and future. What evidence is there to support or oppose this statement in this picture of Istanbul?

splendor, Ottoman sultans (emperors) lived in luxury beyond compare.

The power of the Ottomans reached its peak in the 16th century under the rule of a sultan named Suleiman* the Magnificent. It was not without reason that Suleiman dubbed himself "sultan of sultans, sovereign of sovereigns, dispenser of crowns to monarchs on the face of the earth." His empire stretched all the way from the outskirts of Vienna to Baghdad, along the northern rim of Africa, and along the Red Sea Coast of Arabia.

The Ottoman Empire was so powerful, it seemed it would last forever. But it didn't. In the 17th century the Ottoman Empire began a slow but steady slide downhill. The decline was due to several causes: a failure to keep pace with European science and a failure to bring the army up-to-date. This led to military setbacks, which reduced the Ottomans' boundaries.

By the middle of the 19th century, the Ottoman Empire was termed the "sick man of Europe." Attempts to cure it through reform got nowhere at all. The Turks seemed caught in the web of their own traditions. Many Turks complained that those traditions were too strongly tied to the past.

Outmoded or not, many of these traditions were about to end. So, too, was the Ottoman Empire. An empire built by war was about to collapse under the strain of war. A newer, more modern Turkey was about to take its place.

NORTHERN TIER AND NEIGHBORS

SOVIET UNION

AFGHANISTAN

PAKISTAN

GULF OF OMAN

PERSIAN GULF

Meshed

PLATEAU OF IRAN

IRAN

Shiraz

Isfahan

ELBURZ MOUNTAINS

Tehran

Kuwait City

Hawalli

CASPIAN SEA

Abadan

Basra

KUWAIT

ZAGROS MOUNTAINS

Euphrates R.

Neutral Zone

SAUDI ARABIA

Tabriz

Lake Urmia

Baghdad

Tigris R.

IRAQ

Mosul

Lake Van

Mt. Ararat

SYRIA

Damascus

JORDAN

SOVIET UNION

Beirut

LEBANON

ISRAEL

TURKEY

MEDITERRANEAN SEA

BLACK SEA

Konya

CYPRUS

Ankara

Istanbul

Bosporus

Sea of Marmara

Izmir

Ephesus

AEGEAN SEA

Dardanelles

GREECE

Edirne

BULGARIA

ROMANIA

Miles
0 50 100 150 200 250 300
0   150   300
Kilometers

N E S W

As modern Turkey's first president, Kemal Ataturk wore many hats but shunned traditional Turkish headwear, the fez.

FATHER
OF THE TURKS

HIS STEELY BLUE EYES, his high cheekbones, a brow which wrinkled into ridges when he frowned — these features gave Mustafa Kemal* a determined look. And to his fellow Turks he seemed their greatest leader. As president of Turkey from 1923 to 1938, he picked up the pieces of a tottering, war-shattered country and fitted them into a modern nation.

At the time of Kemal's birth in 1881, Turkey did not even exist. It was then only a part of the Ottoman Empire which stretched eastward into Iraq and southward across North Africa into Libya.

On the day of his birth, Mustafa's father hung a sword on the wall above his cradle. The sword proved to be a sign of things to come. By the time Mustafa had entered his teens, he had decided to become a military man.

At the age of 12, he enrolled in a military school. There he turned out to be such a whiz at mathematics that his teacher named him "Kemal," which, in Arabic, means "perfection." At 18 he went on to a war college in Istanbul, the capital. In 1906 he entered the Ottoman army and swiftly rose through the ranks.

He was serving as a lieutenant colonel in 1914 when World War I broke across Europe. The Ottoman Empire quickly joined with Germany opposing the Allied forces which included Britain, France, and, later, the U.S. The fighting gave Kemal a chance to gain fame for his courage and leadership on the battlefield. But the war did not end happily for the Ottoman Empire, which went down to defeat in 1918.

With the end of the war, the empire collapsed into ruins. The Allied powers occupied the city of Istanbul, and the Greeks, with Allied aid, invaded other Ottoman areas. City and countryside fell into total chaos, and some Turks looked to the military as the only means of restoring order. All the while, many military officers talked openly of forming the Turkish people of the Ottoman Empire into one nation.

These officers needed leadership. Proud, ambitious Mustafa Kemal could offer it. In 1920 a National Congress met, and named Kemal president of a temporary government. In the next two years Kemal's influence spread steadily across his country. Finally, in 1923, he and his supporters created the Republic of Turkey.

Though Kemal claimed to be heading a democracy, he actually ruled with an iron hand. No sooner did he enter office than he started rebuilding Turkey — doing it from the ground up. Hospitals, roads, and power plants were built. New schools were constructed and staffed. A man who had always wanted "to be somebody" had become "somebody," and now he was getting something done.

Kemal enjoyed being powerful, but he always used his power to do what he thought best for his people. Perhaps his hardest job was breaking with many customs developed during the existence of the Ottoman Empire. Kemal lessened the influence of Islam in education and public affairs. He replaced Moslem holy laws with European laws. He urged that Turkish men doff their traditional fezzes in favor of Western hats. He tried to persuade Turkish women to remove their veils. He told them to stop "cringing like animals" when men looked at them in the streets.

One of Kemal's most important reforms — and one of his last — concerned the confusing matter of Turkish names. For centuries, Turks had followed the Arab practice of using only a given name and sometimes a father's name — Mahmud,* son of Ahmed, for instance. Trouble was, Turkey had a great many Mahmuds and Ahmeds, and it was sometimes difficult telling who was who.

So, in 1935, Kemal asked his countrymen to adopt family names in the Western manner — that is, Turkish counterparts to Smith and Jones. Kemal himself dropped his Arab name, Mustafa, and became known as Kemal Ataturk.* The new name meant "Kemal, Father of the Turks."

If another man had taken that name, it would have been a meaningless boast. For Ataturk, it was a simple statement of fact. More than anyone else, he had been responsible for the founding of modern Turkey. More than anyone else, he had kindled its spirit. When he died in 1938, he left behind a people both happier and healthier than he had found them. To this day Kemal Ataturk remains a Turkish hero without equal.

Double-check

Review

1. On what two continents is Turkey located?

2. In one sentence describe the Ottoman palace of Topkapi.

3. The decline of the Ottoman Empire was due to several causes. Name two.

4. Who was modern Turkey's first president?

5. Kemal Ataturk replaced Moslem holy laws with what kind of laws?

Discussion

1. Do you think Turkey's geography and history have made the country more European or more Asian? Explain your answer.

2. In what ways, if any, would Turkey's recent history be different if Kemal Ataturk had not come into power? Using Kemal as your primary example, explain your answer to this question: "Do leaders create history, or does history create leaders?"

3. Why do you suppose Kemal Ataturk urged his people to drop their use of traditional dress and adopt Western dress? Do you think this was a reasonable request? Would you like the President of your country telling you how to dress? Explain your answer.

Activities

1. A group of students might develop a timeline of Turkish history from Greek or Roman times to the present. The timeline could be displayed in the classroom.

2. Some students might research and then draw pictures of Turkish costumes. The completed drawings could be put on a bulletin board under one of two headings: "Traditional Turkish Dress" and "Modern Turkish Dress."

3. The map on page 135 shows the Ottoman Empire to be extensive. Students might do research on other great empires — Alexander the Great's Empire, the Roman Empire, the British Empire — to discover how these empires were built and controlled, why they were not larger, and why they declined. In reports to the class, these empires could be compared with the Ottoman Empire.

Skills

Use the list below and information and maps in Chapters 5 and 9 to do the following on a separate sheet of paper.

Each of the numbered phrases describes the Arab Empire, the Ottoman Empire, or both. For each item, write "A" if the item describes the Arab Empire, "B" if the item describes the Ottoman Empire, or "A and B" if the item describes both empires.

A THE ARAB EMPIRE

B THE OTTOMAN EMPIRE

1. The larger empire.

2. The empire of the eighth century A.D.

3. Included Constantinople.

4. Founded by the Turks.

5. Followers of Islam.

6. Opposed the Allied forces.

7. Baghdad was the capital.

8. The later of the empires.

9. Founded by Arab tribes.

10. Ruled by Suleiman the Magnificent.

11. Conquered Jerusalem in 638 A.D.

12. Led by Omar.

13. Defeated at the Battle of Tours.

14. Termed "the sick man of Europe."

15. Spread the Arabic language across the Middle East.

16. Its scholars translated the ancient Greeks.

Chapter 10

Turkey: Between Two Poles

LIKE OTHER TURKISH TEENAGERS, Zeynep* has studied the history of the Ottoman Empire in school. She enjoys hearing tales of Turkish sultans and the elegant life they led. She is proud of her country's history. But she knows from her reading that a lot has changed since the Ottoman sultans ruled.

The Turkey of today is a nation balanced between the past and future in many different ways. Nowadays most Turks wear Western-style clothing and call each other by Western-style family names. But deep within Turkish culture is a respect for old traditions which stem from an ancient Asian past.

Zeynep's father is a tour guide. He knows more about ancient Turkish history than anyone Zeynep has ever met. Each day he leads visitors through the ruins of once-great cities located near his home. Several times he has taken 15-year-old Zeynep on trips

*Wide boulevards and modern buildings are
not the only scenes in Turkish cities. In
some sections, as in this old quarter of
Istanbul, a sense of the past prevails.*

to show her the ruins he knows best, those at Ephesus.*

The Greek city of Ephesus once sparkled like a pearl on the eastern banks of the Aegean Sea. The Greeks first settled here about the 11th century B.C. At Ephesus they created one of the Seven Wonders of the Ancient World. It was the Temple of Artemis, built about 550 B.C. and named for a Greek goddess of nature.

Over a period of several hundred years, the city fell into ruins, and the ruins were buried by debris. Then, in the 1870's, archeologists began digging in the area to see what they could find. What their spades turned up were the fragments of the original city. Since then, the remains of Ephesus have been uncovered and mostly restored to view.

Tourists now come from halfway around the world to get a firsthand look at these ruins. They stroll down an old marble road, stare up at the bits and pieces of an abandoned temple, and "ooh" and "aah" at what they see. Zeynep also likes to visit Ephesus and hear her father describe how people lived there. Her trips give her a glimpse at a way of life very different from the life she leads.

Zeynep, her eight-year-old brother Hakan,* and her parents live in the city of Izmir, 35 miles to the north of Ephesus. Once Izmir served as a stopping-off place along Asian caravan routes. Now it's a thriving port, Turkey's leading harbor for the shipment of exports such as cotton and dried fruit.

Zeynep's family lives in a modern, two-story house on the outskirts of the city. The house is made of stucco with a roof of bright red tile. It has a living room, dining room, kitchen, three bedrooms, and a bath. On the second floor are two balconies, which seem fittingly placed for a home in modern-day

Turkey. One balcony faces east, and the other faces west.

Zeynep attends ninth grade at a school called Tug-savul.* Like many other schools and streets in Turkey, Tugsavul is named after a military hero — in this case, a former general in the Turkish army. In spite of the fact that Zeynep goes to classes six days a week, she considers herself very lucky. Before the time of Kemal Ataturk, Turkish women rarely went to school at all.

Though her family is of the Moslem faith, Zeynep finds she doesn't have time to practice her religion as fully as she'd like. Her mother still prays five times a day and does not eat until sundown during the holy month of Ramadan. But the other members of the family find it difficult to follow these rules which conflict with work and school.

Their busy schedules also leave them little time to relax as a family group. When they do have time, they try to make the most of it. On some sunny days they take a picnic lunch to one of the many beaches near their home. At other times they go shopping at the old marketplace in the center of the city.

In this old market Zeynep often gets the impression that time is standing still. Vendors push their vegetable carts through crowded walkways just as they have for centuries. Blacksmiths still hammer out ancient farm tools in an unending shower of sparks. On especially hot days Zeynep purchases a cucumber and eats it to cool off. The vendor peels it for her so she can enjoy it while she shops.

In recent years the newer city of Izmir has begun swallowing up the old. Not far from the mosque in the center of the market place are modern buildings with box-like designs of glass and steel. Nowadays many city streets are lined with shiny new

Even in the most modernized lands of the Middle East, donkeys may still be used as beasts of burden, and families may still have to get their water from an ancient source: the local well.

✒ Zeynep rarely goes to parties and never goes out on dates. Her parents think she's still too young.

---

autos — the signs of changing times. Zeynep's parents are proud of their city's "new look," but they are sad to see the older city disappear.

Their outings to the market give Zeynep and her family a chance to shop together. Though their lives sometimes take them in different directions, they are still a close family. They make it a point to follow Turkish custom in the way they address one another. Zeynep's mother, for example, still refers to her husband as *efendim*,* the Turkish word for "my master." Hakan sometimes calls Zeynep *abla*,* the Turkish word for "older sister."

When Hakan was younger, Zeynep helped to raise him. Since she is seven years older than he, she had almost complete authority over him, as Turkish ablas often do. But one day Hakan complained that Zeynep was getting a little too bossy. Since then, she has left him on his own.

Both Hakan and Zeynep are excited about a summer auto trip their parents are planning. They'll travel to eastern Anatolia, where they'll see a performance by Turkish dancers known as whirling dervishes. These dervishes belong to a deeply religious Moslem sect. The purpose of their dances is to attain union with God. Nowadays, however, the dancers perform their ceremony only once a year and at one place — their old monastery in the city of Konya in central Anatolia.

Zeynep's interest in the dervishes is not entirely a religious one. She has been taking dancing lessons for

150

two years. She enjoys Turkish folk dancing, but like many modern Turkish girls she prefers European ballet. By now she is considered a talented ballerina at her school.

Zeynep rarely goes to parties and never goes out on dates. Some of her older friends are allowed to do so, but Zeynep's parents think she's still too young. In some parts of Turkey, girls, whose parents choose their husbands, get married at 15 or 16. But Zeynep thinks that's old-fashioned, and her parents agree. Though she'll ask them to give their blessing to her marriage, she wants to choose her husband for herself.

In the meantime, Zeynep has been planning a career. She loves small children, and she hopes to become a pediatrician (children's physician) some day. If she succeeds, she will be playing her part in the modernization of Turkey. Under Ottoman rule, most women would scarcely have thought of such a thing.

Double-check

Review

1. What building did the Greeks create at Ephesus?

2. What type of heroes are many schools and streets in Turkey named after?

3. Although Zeynep has to attend classes six days a week, she considers herself very lucky. Why?

4. What word does Hakan use to refer to Zeynep, and what does the word mean?

5. What are whirling dervishes?

Discussion

1. Why do you think Zeynep's mother still calls her husband "my master"? Would such a term be used very much in the U.S.? What does this expression say about the position of women in Turkish society?

2. Zeynep's parents are proud of Izmir's "new look" but sad to see the old city disappear. How do you feel about new development in your city? What kinds of development do you approve of, and what further development would you like to see? What kinds of development do you disapprove of? What buildings or areas in your city would you like to see preserved? Why?

3. Why do you suppose the United States and its allies in Europe want Turkey to be their military ally and not to be the ally of the Soviet Union? Do you think it is in Turkey's interest to be an ally of the U.S.? Why, or why not?

Activities

1. Some students might research the power struggle between Turks and Greeks on the island of Cyprus. Then the researchers could divide into teams to debate how political power on Cyprus should be divided.

2. Several students might role-play this scene: While Zeynep's mother's parents are visiting, Zeynep announces she wants to be a pediatrician. Her grandparents hold strongly traditional ideas; her mother feels caught between supporting Zeynep and obediently agreeing with the grandparents; and Zeynep is firm but polite. What happens?

3. Students who like to write might produce an imaginary travelogue, pretending that they have visited Turkey recently and that their job now is to entice others to go there.

Skills

WORLD TRADE IN SOME
MIDDLE EASTERN COUNTRIES, 1975

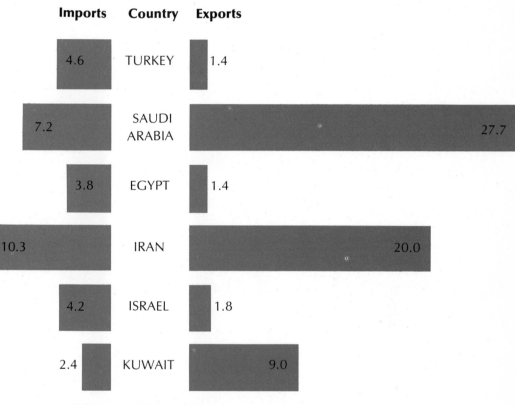

Imports	Country	Exports
4.6	TURKEY	1.4
7.2	SAUDI ARABIA	27.7
3.8	EGYPT	1.4
10.3	IRAN	20.0
4.2	ISRAEL	1.8
2.4	KUWAIT	9.0

(all figures in billions of dollars)   Source: Statistical Abstract of the U.S.

Use the bar graph above and information in Chapter 10 to answer the following questions.

1. What do the numbers on the left represent?

2. What was the value of all Israeli exports in 1975?

3. Which country had the greatest dollar value of imports in 1975?

4. How many countries import more than they export?

5. Which Turkish city's economy is probably affected by the figures in this graph?

Chapter 11

Kuwait:
Rags to Riches

THERE WERE ONLY a few great cities in the old Middle East — among them: Baghdad, Damascus, Mecca, Fez, and Cairo. For every great city, however, there were hundreds of ordinary small towns. Some were market towns where the Bedouins or the local fellahin came to trade. Others were oasis towns where caravans stopped for water and supplies on their way across the desert. Still others were port towns where goods passed in and out of the country, and where the overland caravan routes began.

One such small town, a port town, grew up on the shores of a deep bay on the eastern coast of the Arabian Peninsula, in the northwestern part of the Persian Gulf. The land around the bay was called Kuwait. It belonged to desert people, called Kuwaitis, who had long ago come to the area from central Arabia and decided to settle down.

The sea was the most important influence in the

154

lives of the Kuwaitis. Many Kuwaitis became prosperous merchants and traders. Others were fishermen, pearl divers, sailors, longshoremen, or shipbuilders. Yet the people also lived on the edge of the desert. All the land around the bay was barren sand.

Like much of the Arabian Peninsula, Kuwait was very dry. So drinking water for the townspeople had to be imported — shipped daily down the Persian Gulf from Iraq. The sea provided fish, and there were a few small oasis areas. But outside these areas there were no trees, not even date palms. Except for the fast-fading flowers which blossomed in the desert after the winter rains, hardly a green thing grew anywhere. Like its water, almost all of Kuwait's food had to be imported.

Kuwait was typical of Arabian Peninsula lands in another way: time seemed to bring hardly any change at all. Unlike Egypt, for example, Kuwait had no ancient monuments to attract tourists. Until the 1930's, only a handful of Westerners had ever been in Kuwait. Even fewer Kuwaitis knew anything about the world outside their little homeland.

In the center of the town was a big open market. There herdsmen and tradesmen spread their wares on the ground, and Bedouins brought their camels and sheep to sell. Bedouins could always be seen in Kuwait town, for several tribes roamed the Kuwaiti deserts.

At night the streets of the town were dark. As late as 1940 the houses had no electricity. There were only three or four schools and one hospital. A wall surrounded the whole town, and the wall gates were locked each evening after nightfall. Beyond the wall was nothing but desert.

Except for a few tiny villages, and miles and miles of desert, that town was all that Kuwait had. Surely,

155

Rich Kuwaitis now use autos instead of mules as their "beasts of burden." But many men and women still dress in traditional Arab robes.

of all the Middle Eastern countries, Kuwait seemed just about the last that would ever change. But change came suddenly in the 1940's, bringing undreamed-of wealth and luxury to Kuwait. It was as though a real Aladdin had rubbed his lamp over this tiny desert land.

☆ ☆ ☆ ☆ ☆ ☆ ☆ ☆ ☆

When Ali's father, Bashar,* tells him about the old days in Kuwait, Ali can hardly believe it.

Ali is 14, and he never saw the old town on the bay. By the time he was born, it was much changed, and soon afterward it had all but vanished. The Kuwait that Ali knows has wide avenues crowded with cars and brightly lit at night. It has glass-fronted

156

office buildings, lavish homes, luxurious hotels, and an international jet airport. It has modern shops, and a main thoroughfare — lined with offices, hotels, and department stores — which runs through the middle of the city.

There are parks, too, filled with flowers and shrubs. These are set in the middle of traffic circles or alongside schools and other public buildings. There are many tree-lined avenues. It costs much money to make green things grow in a desert land like Kuwait. Each day trucks must bring the necessary water to each park and each tree.

But the *emir*,* or ruler, of the country is richer now than all the great caliphs of Baghdad put together ever were or ever hoped to be. His people have more than enough money to buy equipment which can turn brackish water, once useless to them, into water fresh enough for growing plants. They don't wait anxiously for ships carrying water from Iraq any more — they "make" their own drinking water instead. Each day millions of gallons of salty water are pumped into a huge new plant. In this plant the water is purified, and the salt and other minerals are removed.

Kuwait has so much money that no one there has to be poor. If anybody needs a house, the Kuwaiti government either builds him one at low cost, lends him the money to build one himself, or rents him one for as little as three dollars a month. If anybody needs a job, the government trains him for one, free, or lends him the money to start a business of his own and then helps him to run it. If anybody, even with all this help, still cannot properly support his family, the government pays him, monthly, the extra money he needs.

There are hospitals of many kinds in Kuwait, and all of them are free. There are more than 300 schools ranging from kindergarten to Kuwait University, and these are free, too. If Kuwaiti girls and boys choose to, they may go to almost any college or university in the world, and the Kuwaiti government pays their tuition and travel costs, and gives them money for living expenses. People who are sick can get the medical care they need, free, even if they must be sent to another country to get it. There are no taxes in Kuwait — the government doesn't need the money.

Kuwait has more doctors for each 1,000 of its people than many other nations have. Almost every family in Kuwait owns a car, and many have more than one. There are well over 200 mosques in the country, most of them new. Beautiful villas and palaces built by members of the emir's family stand in once-lonely desert areas.

How could Kuwait become so rich, and in such a short time? How could a land which had not changed for centuries become, in just a few years, probably the most modern country in the Middle East?

The answer: oil.

Even before 1940, British and American oilmen knew there was oil under Kuwait's sand. World War II put a stop to drilling, however. As soon as the war was over in 1945, more test wells were dug. By 1954, Kuwait earned about 200 million dollars a year from oil. Twenty-five years later, it earned about 11 billion dollars. Money like this goes a long way in a country with under two million people, half of whom aren't even Kuwaitis. They have moved to Kuwait from all over the Middle East looking for jobs.

Ali and his family live about four miles southeast of Kuwait city, in the town of Hawalli.* Once almost everything beyond the city walls was barren desert. Now many modern towns like Hawalli have grown up to the east, south, and west of the capital. Each

158

Thirty-five years ago Kuwait had less than five schools. Now it has more than 300, such as the elementary school shown here.

has its medical clinic, shopping center, schools, theaters, parks, and mosques. Modern highways link the towns with one another and with Kuwait City.

The house in which Ali lives was built in 1958. Like the old Kuwaiti houses, it has a flat roof and is surrounded by high walls. In almost every other way it is Western. It is two stories high and modern in design, with wide windows, a balcony on the upper floor, and a small front garden. The walls are of white concrete, trimmed in bright pink. The house is roomy enough for the whole family: Ali's grandparents, parents, and two sisters.

159

Inside, Ali's house is air-conditioned, as are almost all buildings in Kuwait. It has a modern kitchen and a telephone, and most of its furniture is Western in style. But the family has set aside one room for mostly traditional furnishings such as floor cushions and low tables. In that room the family usually relaxes while sitting around the television set.

On the roof of the house is a storage tank for the family's drinking and cooking water. The water is delivered regularly by truck, pumped into the roof tank, and piped from there into the house.

Ali's family pays much more for every gallon of fresh water they use than do families in the United States. But making salt water drinkable is a very expensive process.

Ali doesn't remember his grandfather's run-down old house in Kuwait City. He was only four years old when the family moved to Hawalli. But the grandfather tells him about it, and Ali has seen houses like it. A few are still left, wedged in between the new buildings, in the oldest parts of the city. Hardly anyone lives in these old houses any more. After 1950, when Kuwait began to earn a lot of money from oil, most people were able to build new homes.

Like many Kuwaitis, Ali's family got the money to build their new house by selling their old one to the government. The emir decided that a good way to share the new oil wealth with the people was to buy at high prices all of the property they were willing to sell. The government needed the land for new buildings and streets. No matter how old or poor a house or shop might be, or how tiny or worthless a plot of land, the owners were sure to receive a good deal of money for it. People who had always been poor suddenly became rich, and families who had always owned much property, but little else, became millionaires.

Double-check

Review

1. The shores of Kuwait are on what gulf?

2. What is an emir?

3. Who pays the costs of university and college education for Kuwaiti students?

4. What has made Kuwait such a wealthy country?

5. Why is there a storage tank on the roof of Ali's house?

Discussion

1. Because the government of Kuwait is so wealthy, it provides free medical care, jobs, low-cost housing, and other benefits for its citizens. Do you think the United States government could or should do the same for all Americans? Why, or why not? To what extent does the United States government provide these things for Americans? Why?

2. How do the ways Kuwaitis and Americans obtain and use water differ? Do you think the Kuwaitis are justified in using their water on parks, flowers, and trees? How would your life be different if you had to pay a much higher price for water?

3. Do you think Kuwait would have a hard time defending itself against a larger country that wanted to seize control of its oil resources? Why, or why not? How have small countries defended themselves in the past? What means might Kuwait use to defend itself?

Activities

1. Some students might draw pictures of what they think the town of Kuwait looked like before the 1940's. Then you could obtain photographs of the modern city of Kuwait and put the contrasting visuals on a bulletin board.

2. Some students might be interested in researching and giving an oral presentation on one of the following processes: (a) desalinizing water; (b) exploring for oil; (c) extracting and refining oil.

3. The Southwestern United States has had water shortages in past years. Students could collect articles and pictures on how water is used in the Southwest and on what efforts are being made to conserve water there. Several students might report to the class on their findings.

POPULATION MAKEUP

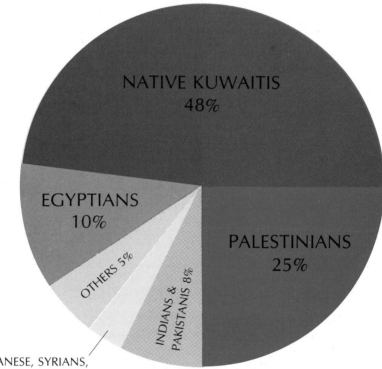

Use the circle graph above and information in Chapter 11 to answer the following questions.

1. What are the two major population groups in Kuwait?

2. What percentage of Kuwait's population is Egyptian?

3. Do native Kuwaitis make up more or less than half of the total population?

4. An American now living in Kuwait would be included in which population group?

5. Which group in the graph probably, before the 1930's, made up a larger percentage of the population than it does now?

Chapter 12

The Impact of Oil

FROM FAR OUT on the Persian Gulf, crews on oil tankers can pinpoint their location by a gleaming tower that rises from a high point on the edge of the Saudi Arabian desert. The lighted tower is the beacon for a university built by oil, for oil, and about oil. Saudi Arabia's University of Petroleum and Minerals is less than 20 years old. But it is already a center for advanced engineering studies in the Middle East.

The university is just one example of how a few oil-rich countries in the Middle East are using some of their new wealth. Education is a key to every country's plans.

Despite the bleak desert location (daytime temperatures sometimes reach 115 degrees Fahrenheit) the university is not a bad place to study. There is no tuition for the Moslem students who come from 19 countries. In fact, the Saudi Arabian government gives each student a monthly allowance for living

*The wealth of Kuwait, based on oil, allows
the government to give away medicine free
if a doctor recommends it. Oil has made
possible a vast revolution in the lives
of people in many Middle Eastern countries.*

expenses. Students have the use of 13 tennis courts, four soccer fields, and an Olympic-sized swimming pool. But they still cannot ignore the desert. Most students wear the traditional white desert robes outdoors. These robes are good protection against the heat and the desert sandstorms that sometimes blow across the campus.

The study of oil is a very serious business in the Middle East. Having the world's largest pool of petroleum underground has propelled the Middle East into an unexpected new role in the world. Oil is the only natural resource some of these countries have, and they want to use it wisely.

In the 1970's, the oil-producing countries banded together to drastically increase oil prices. This group was known as the Organization of Petroleum Exporting Countries (OPEC). Their actions put a huge burden on nations that must import oil, including the U.S. And they brought huge sums of money to the oil-producing nations, especially those in the Middle East. Not every Middle East country is oil-rich. But those that are have collected tens of billions of dollars each year from the rest of the world.

The money has brought new power and prestige. It has also produced new pride and self-confidence in the region. International bankers, businessmen, and diplomats are beating a path to Middle Eastern capitals that they would never have thought of visiting 20 years ago. Oil money has also helped finance the Arab side of the Arab-Israeli conflict.

The "politics of oil" is a term that has been used to describe the use of oil as an international weapon. The Arabs want Israel to give back lands won by Israel in the region's frequent wars (see page 186). In the past, the Arab nations have cut off supplies to countries that support Israel. And they threaten to resume such a boycott in the event of further hostilities in the Middle East. Their hope is that Israel's friends, such as the U.S., will then put pressure on Israel to concede to Arab demands.

To some extent, the Arabs have made progress using oil as a weapon. Some countries in Europe, Asia, and Latin America have taken strong anti-Israeli stands in the United Nations and elsewhere.

But the sudden surge of wealth in the Middle East has created some unusual problems for these oil-rich countries. The Persian Gulf region contains more than half of the world's discovered oil resources. But most of the oil-rich countries contain very few people to absorb the vast amounts of money that are rolling in. It takes more than money to transform a traditional society. It takes industry, trained technicians, an educated and aware populace, markets, and perhaps most of all, time.

Of the oil-rich Middle Eastern nations, only Iran and Iraq have large populations. In the past, they used much of their oil income in projects to raise living standards and build modern economies.

Many years ago, Kuwait began to lend and give money to its Arab neighbors who have not been blessed with oil. In recent years, Saudi Arabia has also developed programs to aid its less-developed neighbors. Some of the oil-rich nations are also spending their oil money to beef up their military strength, buying tanks, planes, radar, and other modern equipment. And some of the nations have given oil money to help advance the cause of the Palestinian refugees who fled from their homeland when Israel was established. Some of this money has even been used to support terrorist activities.

The changes caused by oil wealth are vast, but they are uneven. The pace of change has probably been quickest in Kuwait. There many old social patterns have nearly vanished. One symbol of the new order is the daughter of Kuwait's ruler. She drives her own car and is learning to fly an airplane. Kuwaiti women are probably among the most liberated in the Arab world. As long ago as 1956, a group of them staged a public protest in which they tossed away their veils. Many women today hold important jobs in Kuwait — but this is at least partly because there are not enough men in Kuwait to fill all the jobs.

The rulers of Saudi Arabia seem to be more conservative. They do not want changes to come to their country as rapidly as these changes have come to Kuwait. Saudi Arabia's rulers hope to industrialize without giving up old traditions. Most women in Saudi Arabia remain veiled outside their homes, and Saudi businesses shut five times daily for prayer.

Still the changes have been enormous. In the 1950's, only about 10,000 young people — all boys — attended school. Now there are over 800,000 young people, including some girls, in Saudi Arabian schools.

But the pace of change is uneven. Najeba* is a high school student in the city of Riyadh.* She wears a full-length gray uniform to school. On the street, she is heavily veiled. Inside the all-female school, however, Najeba and her classmates remove the veils. All the men in her family, even her 17-year-old brother, own cars. Gasoline prices are not a problem — premium gas sold for 25 cents a gallon in 1979 in Saudi Arabia. But Najeba does not own a car, or even drive one. Women are not allowed to drive cars in Saudi Arabia.

As the leading Arab nationalist of his time, Egypt's Gamal Abdel Nasser attempted to forge unity in the Arab world.

AN
AWAKENING
OF NATIONS

AGAIN AND AGAIN in the past half century, the force of nationalism has crackled like lightning across the non-Western world. Wherever it's gone, it has made a big difference in the way people think about themselves.

Nationalism is basically the wish for national unity and independence by peoples who share similar languages and customs. Nowhere has this wish been more evident than in the Arab world.

The story of Arab nationalism really begins with another "ism" — colonialism. Colonialism in-the Middle East amounted to long centuries of foreign rule. From the 16th century to the 19th, much of the area was part of the Ottoman Empire and was ruled from Istanbul. Then, as Ottoman power declined in the 19th century, several European powers gobbled up large hunks of Middle Eastern territory for themselves.

Starting in the 1840's, France grabbed up vast sections of North Africa. Not to be outdone, Britain occupied Egypt, and Italy occupied Libya. After World War I, France took control in Lebanon and Syria, and Britain in Palestine and Jordan. The only major area ignored by Europeans was Saudi Arabia (much of which was considered too barren to be useful).

European colonialism did have its benefits. One of them was modernization — the building of roads, irrigation projects, and telegraph lines in many different areas and the development of industries based on Middle Eastern oil.

But as time went on, control by Europe grated and chaffed the Arabs' pride. "Why can't we govern ourselves?" Arabs increasingly asked each other. They staged strikes and demonstrations to back up their demands for self-government.

Nationalism was on the rise, but not all of it sprang from hatred of the Europeans. Often the movement was also inspired by a look backward to the glorious days of the Arab past. A world which had once been united by leaders such as Mohammed and Omar could be united again — or so many Arabs believed. The first step, they thought, was to throw off the shackles of European control.

Their quest for independence bore fruit in three countries — Syria, Lebanon, and Libya — immediately after

World War II. In Syria and Lebanon, nationalist uprisings finally forced the French to leave in 1946. In Libya independence was set in motion by Italy's defeat at the hands of the Allies in 1943. At the end of the war in 1945, Libya came under control of the United Nations, which granted Libya self-rule in 1951.

But sometimes winning independence wasn't so easy. Two cases in point:

Algeria. In the course of more than a century of colonial rule, many French had settled in Algeria where they set down deep roots. So closely linked to their colony were these French people that many of them considered Algeria a basic part of France. But this idea seemed absurd to many Moslem Algerians, who outnumbered European Algerians by 10 to one.

In 1954 Moslem discontent flared into open war. Over the next five years both sides battled with brutal fury. Finally French President Charles de Gaulle said that he would give Algerians the right to determine if they wanted to remain linked to France or have their independence. In 1962 Algerians voted overwhelmingly for independence.

Egypt. Angry outbursts against Europeans were also common in this historic Arab land. Only in this case the Europeans were the British, who took control of Egypt in 1882. In time Arab rioting forced Britain to ease its control. In 1922 Britain granted Egypt independence as a monarchy. Still, the British continued to control the king's purse strings and his foreign affairs as well. Thus Arab nationalists considered their so-called independence a sham.

After World War II the nationalists added a new target to their anger. Now they began condemning the Egyptian monarchy, in part because it was co-operating with the British. More and more Arab nationalists denounced their government as corrupt and unwilling to make reforms. In 1952 their protests overflowed into revolution. Egyptian military officers took control of the government, and the king was driven into exile.

A key figure in this revolution was a young army colonel named Gamal Abdel Nasser.* Dynamic and handsome, Nasser was the son of a humble postmaster in a small Egyptian village. Solemn and studious as a child, Nasser entered Egypt's foremost military academy. While there, he formed a Free Officers Movement, composed of fellow nationalists of his own age. That organization was a major force behind the 1952 revolution.

In 1954 Nasser seized the reins of the revolution he had helped to start. One of his first tasks was to persuade the British to remove their remaining troops in Egypt. The British signed an agreement to that effect in July 1954. Then Nasser got down to the most important business of reform — building Egyptian industries and breaking up the vast estates owned by a small group of wealthy landowners.

Over the years Nasser established himself as a daring politician and a spellbinding speaker. He made many enemies as well as many friends. As his reputation grew, he became the leading spokesman for the Arab nationalist cause. In Nasser the Arab nations had a leader who could spread their ideas around the world.

But did Gamal Abdel Nasser have enough prestige to reunite the Arab world? This became Nasser's great dream. In January 1958, he succeeded in forging a union of Egypt and Syria into the United Arab Republic (UAR).

This seemed the first big step in unifying the Arab world. But it didn't work. In 1961 Syria withdrew over political differences with Nasser. In the last nine years of his life, Nasser worked diligently to promote his ideal of Arab unity. But when he died in 1970 that ideal had not been realized. And it was struck another blow in 1978 when Egypt was harshly criticized by Arab neighbors for signing a peace treaty with Israel.

Although Arab unity has not become a reality, representatives of most Arab nations do meet regularly both to discuss common problems and to carry out joint programs.

Double-check

Review

1. What does the term *politics of oil* mean?

2. Which two oil-rich Middle Eastern nations have large populations?

3. In what oil-producing country has the pace of change probably been quickest?

4. What was the most important reform that Nasser accomplished?

5. In the 1950's, who was the leading spokesman for the Arab nationalist cause?

Discussion

1. Do you see Arab nationalism as a positive or a negative movement? How could it help Arabs? How could it not help them? Why do you think the dream of Arab unity was not realized under Nasser? What kind of leader, or events, would it take for the "dream" to come true?

2. Do you think the other Arab nations were right to ostracize Egypt for signing a separate peace treaty with Israel? Do you think Egypt was right to sign a separate treaty? Explain your answers.

3. Oil resources in the Middle East are limited. Oil reserves there may all be pumped out of the ground in four or five decades if the present rate of production continues. If this happens, what do you think would happen to these oil-producing nations' economies? Do you think the oil-rich countries should slow down their rates of producing oil? Why, or why not? What effect might a cutback in oil production in the Middle East have on the United States? Should this influence the actions of the oil-producing nations?

Activities

1. Some students might research and prepare reports on the current leaders of some Middle Eastern countries, covering such subjects as the leaders' childhoods, how they rose to power, how they view relations with the United States, and how they feel about Arab unity.

2. Some students might draw a map of the Middle East showing which European countries at one time controlled territory there and when each Middle Eastern country obtained its independence.

3. A committee might clip newspaper and magazine articles, political cartoons, and photographs concerning oil in the Middle East and assemble a bulletin board display on the subject.

Skills

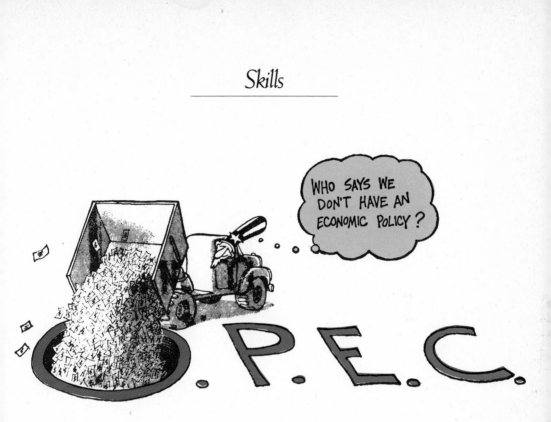

By Auth for The Philadelphia Inquirer

Use the political cartoon above and information in Chapter 12 to answer the following questions.

1. Where did this cartoon first appear?
    (a) newspaper (b) poster (c) textbook

2. Who is the man, and what does he represent?
    (a) an Arab oil magnate, representing oil wealth
    (b) Uncle Sam, representing the United States
    (c) a bank robber, representing the rise of crime

3. Why is the man dumping money down the "O" in OPEC?
    (a) He wants to hide his money from OPEC.
    (b) He is paying OPEC for oil.
    (c) He is giving charity to OPEC.

4. What seems to be the main idea of this cartoon?
    (a) U.S. economic policy is going down the drain.
    (b) The U.S. has raised prices of exports to OPEC.
    (c) The U.S. seems to give all its money to OPEC.

4
ISRAEL

Chapter 13

Promised Land

"THE DESERT SHALL REJOICE," said a Biblical prophet about 700 B.C., "and blossom as the rose." Twenty-seven centuries later, in the land of Israel, the ancient prophesy is coming true. A bright green patchwork of fields and orchards is crowding out the yellow sand and brown rock of the Israeli desert.

Slightly more than 30 years ago, the land was very different. Except for a fertile strip of land along the Mediterranean coast, much of the area was considered too dry and rocky for farming. The hills of Judah, in the center, were badly eroded. Near Lake Tiberias* (the ancient Sea of Galilee) were brackish swamps. The Dead Sea was so salty that no fish could live in it. And the Negev desert, in the south, was as bleak and lifeless as the surface of the moon.

Yet today the Israeli people produce about three quarters of their own food and, in addition, export some. Since Israel's founding in 1948, the amount of food grown in Israel has increased six times. The Israelis have accomplished this by a combination of hard work and modern methods. Where the soil was bad, they added fertilizer. Where the land was dry, they irrigated it. Where swamps made the fields too wet for farming, they drained them.

Israeli farmers drive tractor-powered machines across wide fields. Their cows are milked by machines inside modern barns. Even in the smallest farm settlements there are a clinic and a school. In the larger villages the houses are surrounded by flower gardens and the streets are paved. Some of the farming groups have even started small industries.

All this activity takes place in a startlingly tiny country. Israel rims the Mediterranean Sea for only about 150 miles from north to south, less than the distance between New York and Boston. From east to west, Israel's borders are about 70 miles wide at their widest point. That is less than an hour-and-a-half's drive on a U.S. superhighway.

But what a wealth of geography is packed into this tiny land. From the gentle, rolling hills of the Mediterranean coast to the deep chasm of the Jordan River valley, from the sandy scrubland of the Negev desert to the jutting mountains and broken plains of the north, Israel is a land of surprises.

For most of the year this land is bathed in bright sunshine. From May to October there is virtually no rain at all, and it is sunny for much of the rest of the year. But when it does rain in Israel, it really rains — in heavy torrents for days on end. Then the drooping corn glistens on the stalks and the citrus groves give off the sweet scent of orange blossoms.

*Israeli farmers rely heavily on irrigation
ditches to make their fruit trees thrive.*

"The desert shall rejoice,
and blossom as the rose."

But Israel is more a land of bustling cities than farming villages. Unlike most Middle Easterners, the Israelis are primarily city-dwellers. There are Israeli cities which are thousands of years old, such as Jerusalem, the capital; Hebron*; Jaffa*; Beersheba*; Caesarea*; Acre*; Tiberias; and the port of Haifa.* And there are cities which are new, started since World War I or in the years since the founding of Israel. There are railroads and highways across much of the land. The houses have electricity. The country is prosperous.

David, 15, and his sister, Sarah, 10, live in one of the most modern parts of this modern land. Their home is in Tel Aviv,* the largest city in Israel. It is one of the country's new cities, started in 1909. Next to it is one of the oldest in the world, Jaffa. People consider these two cities, which lie side by side, as one — "Tel Aviv-Jaffa."

Tel Aviv is sunny most of the time — warm in summer and never much colder than 50 or 60 degrees in winter. (This is true of much of Israel. Except for the Negev, Israel has a pleasant climate.) The city faces on the Mediterranean Sea and has a fine beach. It is usually crowded with tourists as well as Israelis. Almost everyone is in Western dress. Cars, buses, taxis, and bicycles jam the streets. The beachfront is lined with large hotels, and the town has many museums, theaters, restaurants, concert halls, and an opera house. Sidewalk cafes dot the major streets.

Tel Aviv has many shops, banks, offices, and factories. About half of Israel's business and industry is carried on in this one city. Downtown Tel Aviv is filled with white apartment houses rising a few stories high.

Many Tel Aviv residents, however, are suburbanites. They have houses in the hills to the north, and travel to work in the city each day. David and Sarah live in one of these suburbs. Their father, a journalist, works for one of the newspapers published in Tel Aviv.

The family's house is one story high and has five rooms, a porch, and a garden. This house is fairly large for Israel, where most houses have no more than three or four rooms. The walls are concrete, painted white. Wood is scarce, as it is in most other Middle Eastern countries, and almost all building is done in concrete, cement, or stone, with stone floors. The house is furnished like ones in Western Europe or the United States.

There are two things David's family doesn't have: a television set and a car. These items are expensive in Israel — they cost about three times as much as in the United States.

David and Sarah were both born in Israel. But almost half of the citizens of Israel came from other lands. Many are Jews from the Arab countries of the Middle East. Many are from Europe. A few came from the United States. An important Israeli law says that: "Every Jew has the right to come to this country as a settler." Of course, many Arabs also live there.

Joseph and Anna, the parents of David and Sarah, were born in Poland. Joseph was David's age when World War II began in 1939. Three years before, his family, like Anna's, had moved to Britain. They were lucky. During the war, all Joseph's uncles, aunts, and cousins died in Nazi concentration camps.

In Britain, Joseph and Anna met and were married. In 1948, when Israel was founded, they went to live in the new country. Many Jews who had been born in Europe went to Israel at that time.

Avraham, who goes to high school with David, was born in Morocco. His father used to own a small shop

*Behind the glitter of Israel's shop
windows lies a quest for a better life for all
Israelis. What does this Tel Aviv street scene
reveal about the Israeli way of life?*

in Fez. Ten years ago, when Avraham was small, the family decided to come to Israel. Many newcomers who had little money settled in farm villages, and in return for their work they were given a place and trained in farming. But Avraham's family, although without funds, was used to city life, so it settled in Tel Aviv. Since coming to Israel, Avraham's father has learned a new trade. He now works in a large fruit-packing plant in the city.

The parents of Benjamin and Zvi,* two friends of Sarah's, were born in Hungary. They came to Israel in 1956, after a revolt in their country against Hungary's Communist rulers. For the first few years, they lived in a farm village. Then they moved to Tel Aviv, where Benjamin and Zvi were born. Their father used to be a high school teacher in Hungary. Now he teaches in a high school in Tel Aviv.

Jews from many parts of the world are still coming to Israel. The Israelis call this immigration into the country *aliyah.** This is a word which means "going up." The Israelis think of the newcomers as people who are coming back to their true homeland.

Aliyah is a Hebrew word, and Hebrew is the language which David and Sarah speak. In Israel, schools teach Hebrew, radios broadcast in Hebrew, and newspapers are printed in and business carried on in Hebrew.

Like Israel itself, Hebrew is both old and new. Most of the Old Testament was originally written in Hebrew. But several centuries before the Romans drove them out of Palestine, Jews had already begun using another Middle Eastern language, Aramaic.* Aramaic was the language that Jesus spoke. Then, during the 2,000 years they lived in other lands, the Jews spoke the languages of those lands. In Germany and Eastern European countries, they combined

Hebrew words with German and other languages to make up Yiddish. Many Jews throughout the world still speak Yiddish.

For all those years Jewish scholars and teachers and other students of the Bible and of the Jewish religion continued to study Hebrew. Jewish religious services were conducted in it. For the most part, however, Hebrew was used just for prayer. No one used Hebrew as an every-day language until modern times. When Israel was founded, the Israelis made this old language the "new" language of their new country.

A modern language may contain hundreds of thousands of words. The ancient Hebrew of the Old Testament, however, contained only about 7,700 words. The Old Testament, of course, said nothing about radios, televisions, trains, jet planes, and all the other modern inventions and gadgets we take for granted.

To meet the demands of the modern world, Israeli scholars had to add countless new words to ancient Hebrew. Some words they borrowed from other languages — *sports* from English, for example. They also gave new meanings to some old Hebrew words. *Hashmal,** for example, is used in the Bible to mean something which is bright or shining, or gives off light. Now the Israelis use hashmal to mean "electricity." *Gafrur** is the modern Hebrew word for a match. In the Bible, gafrur was the brimstone rained down upon Sodom and Gomorrah for their sins.

THE HOLY LANDS

LEBANON

SYRIA

IRAQ

Golan Heights
(Disputed)

Acre

Lake
Tiberias

Haifa

Tiberias

MEDITERRANEAN
SEA

Caesarea

SYRIAN DESERT

Ramat Gan
Tel Aviv-Jaffa

WEST
BANK
(Disputed
Territory)

Jordan R.

Amman

Jerusalem

Hebron

Gaza Area
(Disputed)

Dead
Sea

Port Said

Beersheba

Masada

ISRAEL

Suez Canal

Neutral
Zone

NEGEV
DESERT

JORDAN

Ma'an

SINAI PENINSULA

GULF OF SUEZ

GULF OF AQABA

Aqaba

SAUDI
ARABIA

N

W   E

S

ARAB
REPUBLIC
OF EGYPT

RED SEA

Miles
0   20   40   60   80   100

0   20 40 60 80 100
Kilometers

Ancient mural, about 3,500 years old, shows enslaved Jews forced to carry heavy loads and lay bricks for Egyptians.

CENTURIES-OLD
QUEST

THE ORIGINS OF the modern-day state of Israel go back about 4,000 years to Abraham, a shepherd who left his homeland in present-day Iraq in search of better pastureland. Eventually Abraham made his way into a land called Canaan.* Canaan was located roughly where Israel is today. Choosing a likely spot in this "Promised Land," Abraham set up his tents and dug seven wells. He named one of his new watering places Beersheba. (Beersheba still exists as a flourishing city. An ancient well there is said to be one that Abraham dug.)

But famine struck the new land, and Abraham's descendants left Canaan and migrated to Egypt. Four centuries later, Moses helped lead them back to Canaan.

It took the descendants of Abraham many years to gain control of the land of Canaan. Some two centuries passed before they were able to establish a kingdom there under kings such as David and Solomon. David made the city of Jerusalem his capital, and Solomon built a large temple there to house the Ark of the Covenant (the shrine which held the tablets on which were inscribed the Ten Commandments).

But eventually there was trouble. After Solomon's death, the kingdom split into two states — Israel in the north and Judah in the south. The people of Israel were carried off into slavery by the Assyrians. Years later, Judah was invaded by the Babylonians — who lived in what is now Iraq — and the temple in Jerusalem was destroyed. The Jews rebuilt it and, despite further invasions and conquests, they managed to keep their religion and their way of life alive.

Much later, the Romans took over Palestine. Unlike many other Roman subjects, the Jews refused to submit peacefully to Roman rule. They rose frequently in rebellion against the Romans. Finally the Romans burned Jerusalem and its temple to the ground.

Most of the Jews were driven from the land, although some did manage to stay. Most of those who were driven out settled in Europe or other parts of the Middle East. For centuries they were persecuted and discriminated against in their adopted countries. Often, they were forced to live in *ghettos** (special walled sections of cities). In Eastern Europe, they suffered *pogroms* — murderous attacks by their non-Jewish neighbors. The final horror came when the Nazi Germans slaughtered at least six million European Jews during World War II.

Through the centuries, however, the European Jews never forgot their ancient homeland. Their Passover prayer contained the hopeful phrase, *"Next year in Jerusalem."*

In the late 1800's, many Jews returned to Palestine, then controlled by the Ottoman Empire. After World War I, Britain took over Palestine, and more Jews began immigrating there. Their numbers were considerably expanded after World War II, when many survivors of Nazi concentration camps chose Palestine as their new home.

But the influx of Jews into Palestine stirred anger and resentment among the Arabs who lived there. To the Arabs, the Jews were strangers — people who had come from Europe to take land away from Arabs. Fighting broke out between Jews and Arabs. British troops, opposed by both sides, could not halt the violence. The British turned to the United Nations, which recommended that Palestine be split into separate Jewish and Arab states. The Arabs bitterly opposed the decision, but the Jews welcomed it. (During the fighting, many Arabs who were living in Palestine had become refugees. Many of these people and their children are still living in refugee camps in neighboring Arab countries. Their situation is a primary source of Arab-Israeli bitterness.)

On the afternoon of May 4, 1948, Jewish leaders gathered in a museum near Tel Aviv. There they proclaimed the birth of the state of Israel.

This was the signal for an all-out war to break out between Arabs and Israelis. It was ended by a truce, but three times more in the next quarter century (in 1956, 1967, and 1973) war broke out. Then in 1978, Egyptian President Anwar Sadat said that there had been too much killing. He visited Israel on a mission of peace. Several months later, in the United States, he and Israeli Prime Minister Menachim Begin signed a peace treaty.

Double-check

Review

1. In what year was Israel founded?

2. Almost all buildings in Israel are made of what materials?

3. When Israel was founded, what old language was made the "new" language of the new country?

4. Who helped lead the Jewish people out of Egypt into Canaan?

5. What were pogroms?

Discussion

1. Which of three Jewish immigrants to Israel — one from Boston, Moscow, or Fez — do you think would find living in Tel Aviv the most like living in his or her former city? Which immigrant would find the greatest differences between former and present cities? Why?

2. What problems do any people of differing backgrounds and cultures — such as those in Israel — confront in creating a new culture? How successful do you think the Israelis have been in developing a new culture? What problems have people of different cultural backgrounds faced upon arrival in the United States?

3. An Israeli law gives any Jew the right to settle in Israel. Why do you think this law was made? Should all people have a similar right to settle in the United States? If not, who should and who should not be allowed to settle here? Explain your answers.

Activities

1. A group of students might prepare a large timeline of the history of the Jewish people from the time of Abraham to the present.

2. Some students might look in the Bible for references to places that can be found in present-day Israel. The students could show the rest of the class where these places are located on a map of Israel.

3. Many books have been written about European pogroms and ghettos, Nazi concentration camps, and Jewish immigration to Palestine (later Israel). Some students might read one of these books (either fiction or nonfiction) and write a report on it to share with the class.

Skills

JEWISH HISTORY TIMELINE

c. 1750 B.C.	
c. 1700–1600 B.C.	
c. 1280 B.C.	A. Solomon dies.
	B. Israel is founded.
930 B.C.	C. Moses leads people to Canaan.
922 B.C.	D. Jews suffer pogroms.
	E. Abraham migrates to Canaan.
586 B.C.	F. Temple in Jerusalem is rebuilt.
520–515 B.C.	G. Kingdom is split into Judah and Israel.
70 A.D.	H. Nazis kill six million Jews.
c. 1881 A.D.	I. Romans burn Jerusalem and temple.
	J. Egypt and Israel sign peace treaty.
1917 A.D.	K. Abraham's descendants go to Egypt.
1933–1945 A.D.	L. Britain takes over Palestine.
1948 A.D.	M. Babylonians invade Judah.
1967 A.D.	N. Jews and Arabs fight Six Day War.
1978 A.D.	
c. = approximately	

Chapter 13 describes each of the events listed above. The exact years in which some of the events took place are given in the chapter. For other events, figure out the years from other information in the chapter. For still other events, the only clue to their dates is the order in which they happened. Using the timeline above and by going back through the chapter, try to do the following on a separate sheet of paper.

1. Write the years given above down the left side of your paper.

2. Using the dates and the clues in the chapter, write the letter of each event next to the year in which it happened. (They are *not* in the correct order in the list above.)

Chapter 14

Farmers and Fighters

MANY ISRAELIS are newcomers, but one friend of David's and Sarah's parents, Nathan, has been living in Israel since 1920, when he came there from Poland as a young man. Nathan often tells the young people how in those days there was no country of Israel. The region was still known as Palestine, and Tel Aviv consisted of just a few scattered houses along the shore. The city where Nathan lives now, Ramat Gan,* just east of Tel Aviv, had not yet been built. The Ottoman Empire had just come to an end. Palestine, which had been in the Empire was under British protection.

Nathan was a *Zionist,* which comes from the word Zion, the name used in the Bible for the hill in Jerusalem that 3,000 years ago was the site of the royal palace of King David. Zion was also used as a symbolic name for Jerusalem and the land of Israel.

The Zionists were members of an organization which had been formed in Europe just before 1900.

They remembered that Palestine had been the ancient homeland of the Jews and that, according to the Bible, God had promised the land of Israel to Abraham and his descendants. This is why Israel is often called "the Promised Land." In 1920 the people of Palestine were mostly Arabs. But Zionists such as Nathan had already begun to settle there as early as the 1880's, and to work toward the founding of their own country. This finally happened in 1948, when the United Nations decided that a large part of Palestine should become a Jewish nation called Israel.

Newcomers to Israel now start attending Hebrew schools as soon as they arrive in the country. For older people, it's sometimes very hard. Avraham's parents knew only Arabic, the major language of Morocco. It took them a long time to learn Hebrew. *Sabras** such as David and Sarah are fortunate; they grow up speaking Hebrew. The sabra is a cactus plant which grows in Israel, and the Israelis often use the word to mean people born there. Young Israelis are like sabras, they say, tough on the outside, like the plant's prickly skin, but sweet, like the juice of its fruit, on the inside.

David and Sarah both attend classes six days a week. Their holiday is Saturday, the Jewish holy day. They study geography, history, mathematics, and science, and they must learn English as well as Hebrew. In high school, students may study a third language if they wish, usually French or Arabic.

The Israelis think it important for everyone to know how to grow things, so one of Sarah's required subjects is gardening. In physical education class David usually plays soccer and Sarah, basketball. Other sports are popular, too, especially swimming. All children must learn to swim in elementary school.

One of the books which both David and Sarah

About 1900 many Jews began emigrating to Palestine with the hope of some day making it a Jewish state. It took special pride to create the nation of Israel, the kind of pride illustrated in this photo of a Jewish clean-up crew in 1935.

study in class is the Hebrew Bible. In Israel the Bible is used as a textbook. The Old Testament tells the story of the Jewish people from their earliest days in Palestine and is helpful in teaching the geography and history of Israel.

Sarah will go on to high school in another four years, but some of her friends will not. This is because in Israel, while all elementary schools are free, many secondary schools are not. Many parents cannot afford more education for their children. Students with high marks can go to high school on a scholarship, and many do. David's friend, Avraham, is in high school on a scholarship. He is such a good student that he will probably go on to the Hebrew University in Jerusalem, or perhaps to Tel Aviv University, on another scholarship.

Many young people give up part of their free time to learn farming and other kinds of outdoor work. Most do not plan to be farmers, but they like to feel that they are helping their country. On long holidays David, who belongs to the Israeli Boy Scouts, sometimes spends several days with other members of his troop helping out on a farm. The troop usually goes to a special kind of Israeli farm called a *kibbutz.* *

In Hebrew, kibbutz means "group." A kibbutz is a farm settlement, or village, where families live and work as much as possible as a group. Kibbutz members do not own their own plots of land. All the land and everything else on the kibbutz belongs to the group. Each family has its own house, but all families eat together in one large dining hall. The children visit their parents for part of every day, but they sleep in a special children's dormitory.

A kibbutz tries to provide everything the people need to live — food, clothing, housing, schools, and medical care. Not all the kibbutz members are farmers. Some are cooks. Some are teachers. Some work in

Work on the kibbutz is often difficult — and sometimes dangerous. This Israeli teenager keeps one hand on the steering wheel of his tractor and the other hand near his rifle.

"The soil is good and we are using it to grow things. None of us will be rich here, but we will be comfortable."

the laundry or the clinic. Some take care of the small children while their parents are in the fields.

The first kibbutz farms — or *kibbutzim** — were set up about 1910. Later, after the country of Israel was established, the Jewish settlers banded together to form many more of them. So much had to be done to make the land good for farming — like draining the swamps and irrigating dry areas — that many settlers decided the best way to do it was to work together.

There are hundreds of kibbutzim in Israel today. Some Israelis prefer this kind of life to any other, especially sabras who were born on a kibbutz. Benjamin and Zvi say they would like to try living on a kibbutz some day. This was where their parents first lived when they came to Israel, and their father often talks about it. When they are old enough they plan on joining a special part of the Israeli army whose members also work on kibbutzim.

Rafi is 22 and a worker on an Israeli kibbutz. Rafi's kibbutz is located in territory that was controlled by Syria until it was captured by Israel in the 1967 war.

Two years ago when Rafi was in the Israeli army, he volunteered to work in the special corps which builds fortified farming settlements on Israel's borders as a form of defense. The experience convinced him that farming was what he wanted for his life. After completing his army service, he and three friends volunteered to start a settlement in the newly occupied areas.

Today 23 young men and women work at this settlement. With government financial help and advice, they are raising experimental crops, trying to discover what grows best in the area.

Rafi's group works long, hard hours. They are in their fields before dawn and work until dusk. In the evenings they discuss the next day's work, then visit, or watch television. They have little time for outside social life.

"The soil is good and we are using it to grow things," Rafi says. "None of us will be rich here, but we will be comfortable."

More About the Middle East

In 73 A.D. the hilltop outpost of Masada was the site of a heroic last stand by 960 Jews against the mighty Roman army.

MASADA: FORTRESS OF FREEDOM

IN THE FIRST CENTURY A.D., the area which is now Israel was under Roman rule. Then, in 66 A.D., the Jews revolted. The uprising was crushed, but one lone outpost — Masada* — held out. There 960 men, women, and children resisted the mighty Roman armies for three long years. In the end, they chose death rather than surrender and slavery.

The story of Masada is best known through the writings of one historian of that time: Josephus, a Jew who worked with the Romans. According to his reports, Roman armies built a ramp to the top of the cliff on which Masada stood and attacked the fort with a battering ram and flaming missiles. As the Romans got closer, Eleazar ben Yair,* the commander of the garrison, called his people together. Defeat, he told them, was certain. By dawn the Romans would take the garrison.

But, proposed the commander, there was an alternative to capture. Let us burn our possessions, slay our wives and children. Then let us draw lots, select some from among us to kill the rest. This, wrote Josephus, was what they did. Next day, as the triumphant Romans came dashing through the breach in the wall, they were met only by smoldering ruins and silence — a silence that signified the final defiance.

Josephus was not at Masada at the time of the battle. He got his information through the only survivors of Masada — two elderly women and several children who had hidden in an old well rather than be killed.

But how do we know whether the survivors were telling the truth — and whether Josephus reported accurately? What evidence is there to back up his story? Until recently there was none — and no one really knew whether the story of Masada was fact or fiction.

But a few years ago, an expedition made a careful study of Masada. It dug down through some 2,000 years and several layers of history to uncover the original buildings. The expedition's findings seemed to confirm Josephus' history of the fall of Masada. For example, Josephus had written that the men, after killing their own families, "not being able to bear the grief they were under for what they had done any longer,... laid out all they had in a heap and set fire to it." The diggers, almost 2,000 years later, found small piles of ashes in the rooms used by the defenders of Masada. Among them were the charred remains of children's sandals, water jars, and other household items.

"They then," according to Josephus, "chose 11 men by lot . . . to slay all the rest, . . . and when these 11 had, without fear, slain them all, they made the same rule for casting lots for themselves, that he whose lot it was should first kill the other 10 and, after all, should kill himself." This is backed up by what is perhaps the expedition's most dramatic discovery. In one of the rooms of the fortress, diggers found 11 small, broken-off pieces of pottery, each inscribed in Hebrew with a name. One of the names was "Ben Ya'ir," commander of the garrison.

Of the man chosen in the lottery to be the last to die, Josephus wrote: "And he who was last of all took a view of the other bodies . . . and when he perceived that they were all slain, he set fire to the palace, and with the force of his hand ran his sword entirely through himself." All the buildings excavated were coated with a thick layer of ashes, evidence of a massive fire.

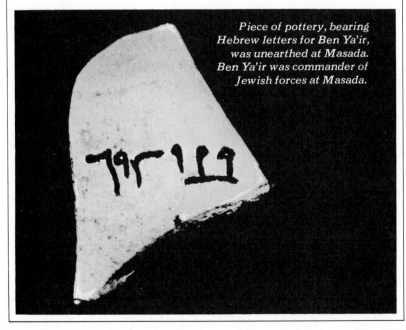

Piece of pottery, bearing Hebrew letters for Ben Ya'ir, was unearthed at Masada. Ben Ya'ir was commander of Jewish forces at Masada.

Double-check

Review

1. Who are Zionists?

2. Which day of the week is Sarah's holiday?

3. What is a kibbutz?

4. The men, women, and children at Masada resisted what armies for three years?

5. How did Josephus get his information about Masada?

Discussion

1. Before 1967 about 15 per cent of Israel's gross national product was spent on the military. In the late 1970's, 30 per cent of the GNP went to military expenses. Why do you suppose the percentage doubled? Do you think the increase was justified? How much of a country's wealth should be spent on the military? On what factors might your answer depend?

2. In Israeli public schools, the Old Testament is commonly used as a textbook. In the United States, religious books are rarely used in public schools. Why is there this difference between the school systems of Israel and the United States?

3. When people join a kibbutz in Israel, they have to give up most of their wealth and valuables to the kibbutz. Property is owned in common by all members. Members do not receive a salary. Instead the kibbutz takes care of the needs of its members. Do you think this is a good system? Why, or why not?

Activities

1. A group of students might interview a person who has visited or lived in Israel. Ask the interviewee to describe life on a kibbutz, urban life, military service, and school life in Israel. Each interviewer could take notes and write a brief report about the interview.

2. A committee of students might plan and prepare a bulletin board display titled "Farming in Israel." They could collect pictures and articles about modern methods of farming, types of farms, irrigation of the desert, and social life on Israeli farms.

3. Other students might research and draw two maps: (a) the British-controlled nation of Palestine; (b) the nation of Israel that was created in 1948.

Skills

EDUCATION IN THE MIDDLE EAST, 1975

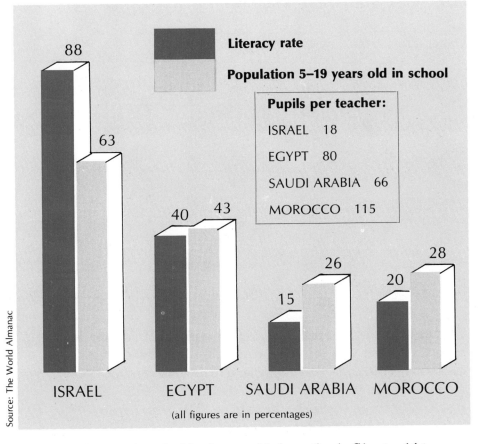

Source: The World Almanac

Literacy rate

Population 5–19 years old in school

Pupils per teacher:

ISRAEL   18

EGYPT   80

SAUDI ARABIA   66

MOROCCO   115

ISRAEL — 88, 63
EGYPT — 40, 43
SAUDI ARABIA — 15, 26
MOROCCO — 20, 28

(all figures are in percentages)

Use the bar graph and table above and information in Chapter 14 to answer the following questions.

1. What do the light bars show? What do the dark bars show?

2. What do the numbers in the boxed table represent?

3. What percentage of Egypt's population was literate in 1975?

4. Judging from the bar graph, is it true that the higher the percentage of a nation's population age five to 19 that is in school, the higher the literacy rate of that nation will be?

5. Do 63 per cent of all Israelis between the ages of five and 19 get free education?

Chapter 15

Joining Past and Present

IN THREE YEARS, when David is 18 and has finished high school, he will join the army, just like Rafi did. In Israel, everyone — even girls if they are unmarried — must spend some time in the army. For boys, it's usually three years. For girls it's a little less. Sarah thinks it will be exciting.

But the army is in the future. Now David and Sarah think more about taking advantage of the city life around them. And in Tel Aviv there are probably more things to take advantage of than in any other city in the Middle East.

In Tel Aviv, David and his friends can see a play or hear a concert at almost any time. Two groups, the Israel Philharmonic Orchestra and the Habimah* theater, are world-famous. Both David and Sarah like movies. Israelis may be the world's champion movie-goers. Each Israeli sees on average 18 films per year, which is about double the U.S. rate. They see a small but growing number of Israeli films as well as many European and American ones, with Hebrew subtitles written out at the bottom of the picture.

In summer the young people often swim. Sometimes the family goes to a resort just south of the city. Sometimes they go on field trips into the Israeli countryside. Schools take students on many field trips each year, for Israelis want young people to see the places important in the history of the Jewish people.

The Jews were the first people to develop a lasting religion based on monotheism.* This word comes from two Greek ones, *monos*, "one," and *theos*, "god," and means belief in One God. Many of the great religions today are monotheistic. When the Jews first expressed this idea, it was new.

Probably the most famous words setting forth this idea are contained in a single sentence from the Book of Deuteronomy.* Deuteronomy is one of the first five books of the Old Testament, which Jews call the *Torah*,* or "law," because they contain the most important laws and beliefs of Judaism. Deuteronomy quotes the last words of Moses, the great leader of the Jews, as he called on his people to remember God's teachings:

"Hear, O Israel, the Lord our God, the Lord is One."

These are words which many pious Jews repeat every day in their morning and evening prayers.

Two other major religions, Islam and Christianity, have adopted the monotheism first developed in Judaism. Moslems are expressing their monotheism when the muezzins, calling the people to prayer five times a day, begin, always, with the words:

"There is no God but Allah, and Mohammed is His Messenger."

Many Christians learn it in this translation of the words of the first of the Ten Commandments:

"I am the Lord thy God. . . . Thou shalt have no other gods before me."

Because the Israelis today come from so many different lands, many different kinds of food are eaten in Israel. Families like Avraham's, from a Middle Eastern country, usually prefer the Arab dishes they ate in the old country. One Middle Eastern food, *felafel,** which is sold on the streets as a quick snack, is popular with almost everyone. Felafel is a garlic-flavored mixture of beans, peppers, and other vegetables, eaten as a sandwich filling.

Families like David's and Sarah's, from European countries, eat food more familiar to Western tastes. Some of their dishes are traditional Jewish ones also eaten by Jews in the United States. *Gefilte** fish, a mixture of fine-chopped fish, onions, eggs, and seasonings, is one of them. *Blintzes,** pancakes rolled up with a filling of cheese or fruit, is another. Many Jews are guided in their diet by strict rules based on Biblical laws. Their food is specially selected and prepared in order to be *kosher,** a word which comes from a Hebrew one meaning "fit" or "proper." Like Moslems, many Jews eat no pork at all. Many also never eat meat at the same meal that they have milk, cheese, butter, or other dairy foods.

Tel Aviv is a fine place to be on Independence Day, the most important nonreligious holiday in Israel. It marks the day in May 1948 when British control over Palestine finally ended and Israel became an independent country under Jewish control. Men and women members of the Israeli army march in parades, and later fireworks and floodlights

Uniformed Israeli army women take a lunch break.

In Israel, nearly everyone must spend some time in the army.

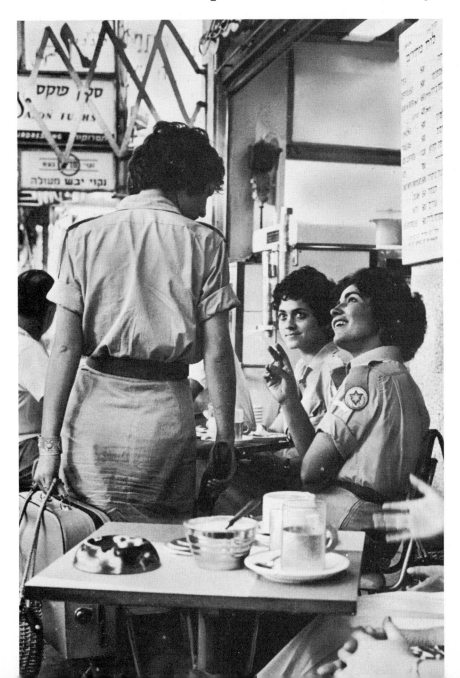

blaze above the rooftops. People join hands to perform the *hora*,* the national dance of Israel, in the streets.

On the first Independence Day after the Arab-Israeli War of 1967, David and Sarah and their parents made their first visit to the "Old City" of Jerusalem. Israel had won control of the Old City during the war. The city was jammed, and one of the most crowded places — as it had been almost a year before, when the war ended — was the Western (Wailing) Wall.

There, next to Sarah and David, stood young sabra paratroopers wearing their dark red berets. There were long-bearded Hasidic* Jews, Israelis whose home had once been Eastern Europe, dressed in the traditional long dark coats and wide-brimmed black hats. There were Yemeni Jews, Israelis who had been born in the Arab country of Yemen and whose clothing was still the long shirt-like garment of the Arabs.

In all their various costumes, they reminded David and Sarah that Jews for many centuries had lived all over the world, far from this land that they always remembered. But now, standing together, they were all united. The past and the present seemed finally to have come together under the flag of Israel.

Only in a few places, such as the city of Jerusalem (right), do Arabs and Jews actually meet to discuss their differences. As the raised eyebrows and drawn faces of these two men indicate, they have a lot more talking to do before their differences can be solved. After reading this book, do you think their differences can be solved peacefully?

Double-check

Review

1. What is the Torah?

2. Why are many different kinds of food eaten in Israel?

3. What date does Independence Day in Israel mark?

4. What is the national dance of Israel?

5. Where had the Hasidic Jews' homes once been?

Discussion

1. In what ways are Islam, Judaism, and Christianity similar religions? What factors might account for these similarities? Do you think that the similarities will eventually help Jews, Arabs, and Christians to live together peacefully in the Middle East? What do you predict will happen among these groups in the next decade? What would you like to see happen?

2. Arabs living in Israel constitute a large minority. Some critics of Israel say the Arabs there are sometimes discriminated against in much the same manner that minorities in the United States have been discriminated against. Why do you think that this discrimination problem might exist in Israel? What could be done about this problem?

3. Do you think Middle Eastern countries will become more, or less, "Westernized" in the future? Why? What contributions have the people of the Middle East made to our culture and way of life? What contributions do you think they will make in the future?

Activities

1. Some students might draw political cartoons that depict relationships between various Jewish and non-Jewish peoples living in Israel.

2. The Jewish people of Israel have many special recipes which have been handed down from generation to generation. Some students might obtain these recipes and prepare dishes which the class could sample. Other students could report on the foods of other Middle Eastern countries, or do research on the dietary laws of Jews and Moslems.

3. Some students might make a bulletin board display on urban life in Israel, using newspapers and magazines as sources for the pictures and the caption information.

Skills

THREE COUNTRIES' ARMED FORCES PERSONNEL
1972–1975

Numbers in thousands

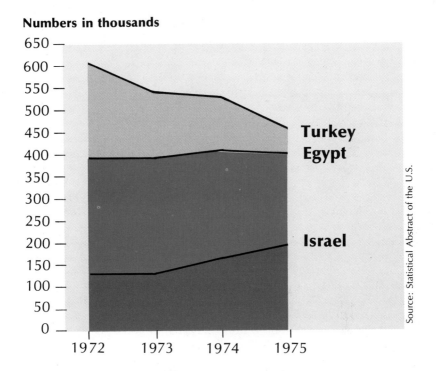

Use the line graph above and information in Chapters 13, 14, and 15 to answer the following questions.

1. What do the numbers on the left of the graph represent? How many years does the information on this graph cover?

2. What country had a steady increase in armed forces personnel from 1973 to 1975?

3. How many members of the armed forces did Turkey have in 1972?

4. When, and between which countries, were the numbers of armed forces personnel most nearly the same?

5. What might explain the increase in armed forces personnel in Israel from 1973 to 1975?

EPILOGUE

A LOOK
AHEAD,
A LOOK BEHIND

THE STRUGGLE between Arabs and Israelis and the Is-
lamic reawakening make headlines almost every day.
The daily life of Middle Easterners is rarely news.
Yet, as we have seen, there is much more to life in the
Middle East than stories which make headlines. True,

the Arab-Israeli dispute and the Islamic renewal are close for some Middle Easterners, but not for all.

It would be a mistake to think that all of the people of Israel live one way of life, and all of the people of the Moslem countries another. Despite the divisions of religion and politics, there is no rigid line between the two peoples. Before 1979, Yasmine, in Teheran, would have had more in common with David in Tel Aviv than with Hassan in his "house of hair" in the Arabian desert. Avraham's father, who came to Israel from Fez in Morocco, might feel more at home with Khaled's father, who lives in Fez, than with David's father who came to Israel from Poland by way of Britain.

Obviously, all Israelis are not alike. Some are religious and some aren't. Some have their roots in the Arab Middle East; some, in Eastern Europe; and some, in Western Europe and the U.S.

If this diversity is true for Israel, it is even truer for the Arab lands. Depending on where they live and how they earn their living, Arab peoples follow ways of life that are sharply different from one another. Kuwaitis, for example, are mostly business people or government workers. Most Egyptians, except for those who live in the large cities, are farmers, tilling the land in almost the same manner as their ancient ancestors. And the Bedouins of the Arabian and Saharan deserts know little of either farming or business.

While the Arab and Ottoman empires were at their heights, most of the Arab and Moslem countries were united under a single ruler. Now that is changed. There are many independent countries with many different kinds of governments. A few are republics; there the people elect their government officials democratically. Many others have far less democracy, or

Almost everyone's life is changing, sometimes rapidly, usually slowly — but changing nevertheless.

Egyptian fellahin inspect model of a U.S. space capsule.

none at all. They may be called republics, but one man or a small group of men have all the real power. Others are monarchies ruled by a king, sultan, sheik, or emir. He may, or may not, share some of his power with his people.

All of these differences have led to disagreements at times. In recent years many of the Arab countries have had serious quarrels with one another. Often the Arab republics have been at bitter odds with the Arab monarchies. But these divisions are not new. Throughout the centuries, the peoples of the deserts, the farmlands, and the towns have not mixed well together. The Bedouins have generally considered themselves better than the fellahin and the city Arabs. Until modern times the settled people have feared the tough and warlike desert tribesmen.

Yet the Arab countries maintain a bond which no differences seem able to break. These countries have a common culture, and this is one of the strongest ties that can bind people together.

Culture is a term that is often used, but little understood. What does it mean? It includes people's customs, the way they look at life and the world, the beliefs that they hold, their language, the way they express themselves in art and literature. Almost all the people of the Middle East are Moslems, and their attitudes, their arts, and their customs almost all stem from Islam.

The way Middle Easterners build their houses, for example, differs only slightly from country to country. Most houses — even "houses of hair" — have one thing in common: they have been designed to keep the lives of women as private as possible, and to shield the family from the eyes of strangers. Outside the large cities, loyalty to one's clan or tribe is one of the most important things in life. In some places, as in

212

the Arabian desert, it is often more important than loyalty to government.

Most Middle Easterners speak the same language, Arabic. The kind of "every-day" Arabic which Munir and Ali speak in Cairo is quite different from that which Khaled speaks in Fez. In fact, Munir and Ali would have a hard time holding a conversation with Khaled. But the "formal" Arabic in which all three pray — the old, "classical" Arabic in which the Koran is written — is the same. The Koran binds the three young people together. So does the Arab past, with all the Arab works of poetry, philosophy, and science which were written in the language of the Koran.

The Islamic cultural bond is one of the most important things about the Middle East. But another is the change which is now taking place in all of them. Almost everyone's life is changing, sometimes rapidly, usually slowly — but changing nevertheless.

In some countries, the change is toward Westernization. There is something new almost everywhere. Even a single transistor radio in a remote Arab village, even a truck on the horizon of a desert where once only Bedouins and camels walked, makes a difference.

In other countries, the trend toward Westernization has been challenged by a renewed interest in traditional Islamic laws and customs.

It is still unclear how these conflicting trends will affect the countries — and the people — of the Middle East in the coming decades. But it does seem clear that whatever happens will be interesting and will have great impact on the rest of the world.

Pronunciation Guide

The following system translates each syllable into the near-est common English equivalent. Syllables set in capitals are ac-cented. Principal sound equivalents are:

a (as in cat)
ah (as in odd)
aw (as in lawn)
ay (as in ale)
e (as in silent)
ee (as in eat)
eh (as in end)
g (as in go)
i (as in charity)
ie (as in ice)
ih (as in ill)
j (as in John)
k (as in keep)
o (as in connect)

oe (as in hoe)
oh (as in old)
oo (as in too)
or (as in for)
ow (as in out)
s (as in sit)
sh (as in ship)
t (as in tin)
th (as in then)
u (as in circus)
uh (unaccented a as in sofa)
ur (as in urn)
y (as in yet)
z (as in zebra)

Abdullah — ahb-DUHL-uh
abla — AH-bluh
Acre — AY-kur
Ahmed — AH-mehd
al-Azhar — ahl-AHZ-hahr
aliyah — ah-lee-YAH
Amina — uh-MEE-nuh
Aramaic — ar-uh-MAY-ihk
Ararat — A-ruh-rat
Aswan — ahs-WAHN
Ataturk — AT-uh-turk
Ayatollah Ruhollah Khomeini — ie-ah-TOHL-luh
 roo-HOHL-luh hoe-MAY-nee

Babylonians — bab-uh-LOH-ny-uhnz
Baghdad — BAG-dad
Bashar — buh-SHAHR
Bedouin — BEHD-uh-wuhn
Beersheba — beer-SHEE-buh
blintzes — BLIHNT-sihz
Bosporus — BOS-puh-ruhs
Byzantine — BIHZ-'n-teen

Caesarea — seh-suh-REE-uh
Cairo — KIE-roh
caliph — kah-LEEF
Canaan — KAY-nuhn
cuneiform — kyoo-NEE-uh-fohrm

Damascus — duh-MAS-kuhs
Dardanelles — dahr-duh-NEHLZ
Deuteronomy — dyoo-tuh-RAHN-uh-mee

efendim — eh-FEHN-dihm
Eleazar ben Yair — ehl-yuh-ZAHR behn yah-EER
emir — ih-MIHR
Ephesus — EH-fuh-suhs
Euphrates — yoo-FRAY-teez

Fatimah — FAH-tee-muh
Fawzia — fow-ZEE-yuh
felafel — f'-LAH-fuhl

fellahin — FEHL-luh-heen
Fouad — FOO-ad

gafrur — guh-FROOR
Gamal Abdel Nasser — guh-MAHL AHB-d'l NAHS-uhr
gefilte — guh-FIHL-tuh
ghettos — GEH-tohz
Gibraltar — jih-BRAHL-tuhr

Habimah — hah-BEE-muh
Haifa — HIE-fah
Hakan — HAH-kahn
Hamid — HAH-mihd
harem — HAR-uhm
Haroun — hah-ROON
Hashem — HAH-shehm
hashmal — hahsh-MAHL
Hasidic — hah-SEE-dihk
Hassan — HAH-suhn
Hawalli — huh-WAH-lee
Hebron — HEE-bruhn
hegira — HEH-gee-rah
hora — HOH-ruh

Istanbul — ihs-tan-BOOL

Jaffa — JAH-fuh

kebab — keh-BAB
Khadija — khuh-DEE-jhuh
Khaled — KHAH-lehd
kibbutz — kihb-OOTS
kibbutzim — kihb-oot-SEEM
Koran — KOH-rahn
kosher — KOH-shuhr

Mahmud — MAH-mood
mahr — MEH-hehr
Marmara — MAHR-muh-ruh
Masada — muh-SAH-duh
medina, Medina — muh-DEE-nuh
Menes — MEE-neez
minaret — mihn-uh-REHT

monotheism — MAH-nuh-thee-ihz-uhm
mosque — MAHSK
muezzin — MWEHZ-'n
Munir — moo-NEER
Murrah — MOOR-uh
Mustafa Kemal — MOOS-tuh-fuh KEH-mahl

Najeba — na-JEE-bah

oasis — oh-AY-suhs
Omar — OH-mahr

pharaoh — FEH-roh

Ramadan — RAH-muh-dahn
Ramat Gan — ruh-MAHT GAHN
Riyadh — ree-YAHD

sabras — SAH-bruhs
Safiya — sah-FEE-yuh
Salamah — suh-LAH-muh
shadoof — shuh-DOOF
Shah Mohammed Riza Pahlevi — shaw mo-HAH-mud
   REE-zuh pah-LAH-vee
sheik — SHEEK
Sinai — SIGH-nigh
Suleiman — SOO-lay-mahn
Sumerians — soo-MEH-ree-uhnz
Syed — SY-ihd

Teheran — TEH-huh-RAN
Tel Aviv — TEHL ah-VEEV
Tiberias — tigh-BEE-ree-uhs
Tigris — TIGH-grihs
Topkapi — TOP-kuh-puh
Torah — TOH-ruh
Tugsavul — TOO-suh-vool

Yasmine — yas-MEEN

Zeynep — ZAY-nehp
zurkhaneh — zer-KAH-neh
Zvi — ts'-VEE

Index

*Photograph

PHOTO AND ART CREDITS: 6, Carl Frank • 7, Camera Press/ PIX • 10, De Wys • 20, The University Museum, Philadelphia • 28, Paul Conklin/PIX • 32, Bruno Barbey/MAGNUM • 34, Edinburgh University Library • 41, De Wys • 45, (top) Arabian American Oil Company; (bottom) Leni Sonnenfeld from Monkmeyer • 47, Tor Eiseland from Black Star • 53, Gunther Reitz/PIX • 57, Three Lions • 62, Carl Frank • 65, De Wys • 70, The Bettmann Archive • 77, Henri Cartier-Bresson/MAGNUM • 86, De Wys • 89, Leni Sonnenfeld from Monkmeyer • 95, Inge Morath/MAGNUM • 100, Black Star • 101, UPI • 102, (top) Sheila Turner; (bottom) Wide World • 103, Marc Riboud/MAGNUM • 104, (top) Gunther Reitz/PIX; (bottom) Leni Sonnenfeld • 105, (top) Camera Press/PIX; (bottom) Gunther Reitz/PIX • 106, Camera Press/ PIX • 107, (top) Photo Researchers; (bottom) Frank Fishbeck from Black Star • 108, Leni Sonnenfeld from Monkmeyer • 109, Carl Frank • 110, Dorka Raynor from Nancy Palmer Photo Agency • 111, (top) Photo Researchers; (bottom) Carl Frank • 112, (top) Gunther Reitz/PIX; (bottom) Leni Sonnenfeld from Monkmeyer • 113, (top) Sheila Turner; (bottom) Paul Conklin/ PIX • 114, (top) Carol Gootter from Black Star; (bottom) Rene Burri/MAGNUM • 115, UPI • 116, Carl Frank • 117, Three Lions • 118, Camera Press/PIX • 119, (top) Pictorial Parade; (bottom) Gunther Reitz/PIX • 120, Carl Purcell, AID • 121, (top) UPI; (bottom) Sheila Turner • 122, (top) Leni Sonnenfeld; (bottom) Three Lions • 123, Standard Oil Company (New Jersey) • 124, Camera Press/PIX • 125, Henning Christoph from Black Star • 126, Elliott Erwitt/MAGNUM • 127, (top left) Israel Information Services; (top right) Gunther Reitz/PIX; (bottom) Photo Researchers • 128, (top) Leni Sonnenfeld; (bottom) Camera Press/ PIX • 129, Marc Riboud/MAGNUM • 130, Capezza from Monkmeyer • 131, (top) Sheila Turner; (bottom) Leni Sonnenfeld from Monkmeyer • 132, Paul Conklin/PIX • 137, Black Star • 140, Brown Brothers • 146, Gunther Reitz/PIX • 149, Marion Wolcott/ PIX • 156, 159, Bruno Barbey/MAGNUM • 164, Three Lions • 168, Rene Burri/MAGNUM • 174, 177, Leni Sonnenfeld from Monkmeyer • 180, Camera Press/PIX • 184, Photographic Archive of the Jewish Theological Seminary of America, New York • 191, New York Public Library • 193, Leni Sonnenfeld from Monkmeyer • 195, 197, Jewish Theological Seminary • 203, Camera Press/PIX • 205, W. Braun/PIX • 208, Henning Christoph from Black Star • 209, Bruno Barbey/MAGNUM • 211, UPI • Cover, T. Hopker/WOODFIN CAMP.
MAPS by IRMGARD LOCHNER.